THE EPIC VOICE

HAMPSHIRE STUDIES IN THE HUMANITIES

THE EPIC VOICE

Essays by
John Maier
Robert Alter
Stanley Lombardo
Wendy Doniger
Tomás Ó Cathasaigh

Edited by
Alan D. Hodder
Robert E. Meagher

PRAEGER   Westport, Connecticut
                              London

Library of Congress Cataloging-in-Publication Data

The Epic voice / edited by Alan D. Hodder and Robert E. Meagher.
    p. cm.—(Hampshire studies in the humanities)
    Includes bibliographical references.
    ISBN 0–275–97604–1 (alk. paper)—ISBN 0–275–97605–X (pbk. : alk. paper)
    1. Epic literature—History and criticism. I. Hodder, Alan D. II. Meagher, Robert E. III. Series.
PN56.E65E666 2002
809′.132—dc21   2001058048

British Library Cataloguing in Publication Data is available.

Copyright © 2002 by Alan D. Hodder and Robert E. Meagher

All rights reserved. No portion of this book may be
reproduced, by any process or technique, without the
express written consent of the publisher.

Library of Congress Catalog Card Number: 2001058048
ISBN: 0–275–97604–1
       0–275–97605–X

First published in 2002

Praeger Publishers, 88 Post Road West, Westport, CT 06881
An imprint of Greenwood Publishing Group, Inc.
www.praeger.com

Printed in the United States of America

The paper used in this book complies with the
Permanent Paper Standard issued by the National
Information Standards Organization (Z39.48–1984).

P

Copyright Acknowledgments

The authors and publisher gratefully acknowledge permission for use of the following material:

Excerpts from Stanley Lombardo, trans. *Iliad*. Indianapolis, IN: Hackett Publishing, 2000.

Excerpts from Stanley Lombardo, trans. *Odyssey*. Indianapolis, IN: Hackett Publishing, 2000.

From *The Divine Comedy* by Dante Alighieri, translated by John Ciardi. Copyright 1954, 1957, 1959, 1960, 1961, 1965, 1967, 1970 by the Ciardi Family Publishing Trust. Used by permission of W.W. Norton & Company, Inc.

Excerpts from Cecile O'Rahilly. *Táin Bó Cúailnge: Recension I*. Dublin: Dublin Institute for Advanced Studies, 1976.

Photo of the *Male Harp Player of the Early Spedos Type*. The J. Paul Getty Museum, Malibu, California. © The J. Paul Getty Museum.

In order to keep this title in print and available to the academic community, this edition was produced using digital reprint technology in a relatively short print run. This would not have been attainable using traditional methods. Although the cover has been changed from its original appearance, the text remains the same and all materials and methods used still conform to the highest book-making standards.

TABLE OF CONTENTS

INTRODUCTION
· 1 ·

GILGAMESH
· 15 ·

DAVID
· 53 ·

ODYSSEY
· 75 ·

RAMAYANA
· 101 ·

TÁIN
· 129 ·

INDEX
· 151 ·

ABOUT THE CONTRIBUTORS
· 155 ·

MAPS
Epic Homelands · vi
Ancient Sumer · 18
Davidic Kingdom · 56
Ancient Mediterranean · 78
Ancient India · 104
Ancient Ireland · 132

EPIC HOMELANDS

INTRODUCTION

HAMPSHIRE STUDIES IN THE HUMANITIES

Across the country—from community colleges to the most select liberal arts colleges and universities—there has been and continues to be a marked return to the thoughtful and critical consideration of core, seminal texts in the humanities. In this process, some institutions have exhumed the traditional western canon, the notorious "great books," while others—instructed by the curricular debates of the past several decades—have chosen a wider, more inclusive net. This has led to a plethora of core courses and core curricula, often wildly interdisciplinary in scope and intent, and yet most commonly taught by junior or adjunct faculty recently trained in a single discipline. The results, by all reports, have been mixed.

In this moment of both experimentation and return, the humanities faculty of Hampshire College may well have something valuable, if not unique, to offer. For the past thirty years, within always limited resources, our curriculum has been equally committed to preservation and experimentation. From the start, our work has been consistently, even die-hard, interdisciplinary, comparative, multicultural and collaborative, while our students, both in their coursework and in their independent projects have learned to take for granted the expectation that they will work predominantly from and with primary sources.

The aim of the Hampshire Studies in the Humanities is to form each year a collaborative core of faculty and students from Hampshire and our sister institutions in the Five-College Consortium—Amherst College, Mount Holyoke College, Smith College, and the University of Massachusetts—and to bring into our midst five senior visiting scholars of international stature to offer public lectures and to participate in model interdisciplinary seminars focused on seminal texts in the humanities. Finally, from each year's lectures and seminars we produce a text, which is both a monograph and a veritable "course-in-a-book," one which we hope will prove to be a valuable curricular resource for colleges and universities throughout the country.

The core of each text is comprised of essays written by our five visiting scholars, essays based on the public lectures and seminars which they have offered throughout the term. In each essay, a senior scholar draws upon decades of learning and thought to open the reader's mind to the fullness of the work at hand. It is all about "getting to the heart of the text" as each scholar has come to understand it, not advancing any personal agenda or applying to the text a narrow scholarly perspective. These essays are thus intended as heuristic guides to the text as a whole—illuminating, provocative, infectious—but not exhaustive nor for that matter comprehensive. We might imagine each essay accompanying its companion text in a time capsule, explaining to readers of the future why these particular texts should never be lost and how to begin reading them so as to discover their unique legacy. Consistent with the pedagogical aims of the series, we have tried to keep to a minimum footnotes and scholarly apparatus. However, the editors have compiled a series of maps, time-lines, study questions, and discussion points, often from material introduced in the seminar meetings, to facilitate access to the texts.

THE EPIC VOICE, the first course offered under the auspices of the Hampshire Studies in the Humanities, is focused on five ancient epics: the Mesopotamian *Epic of Gilgamesh*, the Hebrew *David Story* from 1 and 2 Samuel and 1 Kings, the Greek *Odyssey* of Homer, the Indian *Ramayana* of Valmiki, and the Irish *Táin Bó Cúailnge*.

EPIC, MEMORY, AND HUMAN IMAGINATION

There has always been more than one way to travel. It was the physician Hippocrates who suggested that thinking is, as he put it, the soul's trek abroad. To be sure, the *curriculum* (literally "racecourse") laid out in this volume, while retracing some familiar turf, will take most any thinking mind, young or old, far afield, into untrod lands and legends. Indeed, in an age of collapsed time, when the proverbially disqualifying "hill" is approached at thirty, and when "ancient history" is likely to refer to the previous century, the study of Bronze and Iron Age epics will strike many readers as remote—but not for long, not once those same readers begin to read on. Robert Alter, for example, one of the preeminent literary critics of our time, finds the Story of David, as told in the biblical books of Samuel, to be "altogether one of the greatest stories we have," as contemporary and compelling as any we are likely to encounter on any bookshelf worth browsing. And the other four scholars featured in this volume would and do say much the same of the stories they explore in depth here. These are stories as much for today as for yesterday. It is our loss when we overlook them. Goethe, in several of his more famous lines, suggested how we might measure that loss:

> Wer nicht von dreitausend Jahren
> Sich weiss Rechenschaft zo geben
> Bleib' im Dunkeln unerfahren
> Mag Tag von Tage Leben.

> *He who cannot give account to himself of three thousand years— May he stay in darkness, inexperienced; may he live from day to day.*[1]

For generations as committed to "life experience" as those afoot today, charges of inexperience cannot be taken lightly. The truth, however, is that the literary horizon has expanded since Goethe wrote these lines, and the human stakes are, if anything, higher. By even a modest reckoning, five, not three, thousand years must now be accounted for. And so that is where our stories here begin, with Gilgamesh, King of the Sumerian city of Uruk, nearly five millennia ago. More to the point, his story reads as a template of our own; beyond engaging, it is inescapable. It is not enough to chant the cliché that those who forget the past are doomed to repeat it: the truth is that the past mostly repeats itself whether we remember it or not. Remembering serves another purpose.

"Great is the power of memory," wrote Augustine of Hippo in his *Confessions,* "something to hold in awe... profound, limitless, beyond counting. And this something is the mind. It is simply what I am."[2] Mind—Memory—Humanity: these are equivalent for Augustine. The one is the door to the other; and together they comprise the inner space in which we live and discover ourselves. Outside there is only darkness, darkness without redress, the darkness of oblivion, inexperience, and immediate pleasure and pain. Memory, from another ancient perspective no less urgent than Augustine's, is a matter of life and death, a matter of sheer survival. Any full account of five thousand years of humanity must reckon with these words from the Egyptian Book of the Dead

> That which can be named exists.
> That which is named can be written.
> That which is written shall be remembered.
> That which is remembered lives.[3]

Gilgamesh, David, Odysseus, Rama, and Cú Chulainn—all live because they are remembered and are remembered because their names and stories have been written. Nothing of them, however, not even their names, would have been written, unless they had already lived in the imaginations of, and been formed into words by, others who had somehow witnessed their deeds. Heroes need poets and poets need heroes. Without the inspiration of bold lives and deaths, poets go mute; and, without poets, everything bright dims and dies forever.

The task of modern education, suggested C.S. Lewis, now decades ago, is not to cut down jungles but to irrigate deserts. The inner deserts he had in mind are the legacy of long erosion, the erosion of imagination, the erosion of memory. The epics discussed in this volume, however, are nothing less than jungles, rampant with wondrous life-forms, teeming with endangered species—gods, demons, monsters, heroes, tastes, visions, sounds, fears, and hopes almost lost—all willing to inhabit, possess, and reforest an open mind. The voice in each of them we have called THE EPIC VOICE, the voice of great and ancient stories. At first the voice of each epic may seem distant, even exotic, but with the guidance of the essays in this volume and with both private mulling and shared discussion, the voice becomes recognizably human. After all, wrote the Roman playwright Terence: Homo sum: humane nil a me alienum puto ("I'm a human being. When I think about it, nothing human is really foreign to me.")[4]

EPIC, ORALITY, AND THE HEROIC AGE

It must be acknowledged here at the outset that in corralling all five of the far-flung works discussed in the following pages under the generic category of epic, the editors have been motivated, in some small degree, by pedagogical convenience. The biblical story of David, in particular, sits somewhat uneasily in the place we have prepared for it in this collection. As a work composed primarily in prose, not poetry, and perhaps within a generation or two of the events it recounts, the David story clearly departs to some extent from the more typical path associated with the traditions of oral poetry. We are, of course, on firmer ground in construing the other works in this way, but even in such cases, we must proceed with at least a modicum of caution. While many comparativists today would not hesitate to characterize the *Gilgamesh*, the *Odyssey*, the *Ramayana*, and the *Táin* as notable examples of the epic genre, it is important to remember that the conception we have of this genre derived in the first place from the oral traditions of ancient Greece, specifically the great works of the *Iliad* and *Odyssey* ascribed to Homer, and was only much later extrapolated to the heroic poems of other ancient civilizations. In view of this critical legacy, it is perhaps not surprising that even today we are sometimes inclined to think of the *Iliad* or the *Odyssey* as the paragon of the epic form. But there is little historical warrant for such a view unless we conceive of literary genres in some transcendent or archetypal way. The real lesson to be gleaned from our observation about the conventional critical privileging of Homer is rather that literary genres narrowly conceived are as much the creatures of particular traditions, particular cultures, and particular histories, as the texts through which they are embodied.

The English word "epic" itself derives from the Greek *epos*, which originally meant simply "word" or, more generally, "tale" or "song." It was only with Plato in the fourth century B.C.E. and, more influentially, his disciple Aristotle that the plural form of this word, *epē*, was used in the generic sense as a term to distinguish epic poetry from other forms of verbal art.[5] In the *Poetics*, a treatise on classical literature that had an incalculable influence on subsequent Western thinking about literary genres, Aristotle distinguished three main literary forms—tragedy, epic, and lyric poetry—and, in doing so, elevated epic poetry to a place of significance second only to tragedy. Although Aristotle's main objective in this work may well have been simply to describe the shape of classical literature as he saw it, one of its main consequences for later Western writers was to bestow upon these particular forms a special authority and prestige. By the Renaissance, epic had eclipsed even tragedy in importance, thus assuming the most exalted station in Western theories of literary art. It was in part because of the homage paid to epic by Aristotle and later writers that a rich tradition of literary epic grew up in the Western world around the epics of the Homeric tradition. The difference, of course, between Homer and his various literary descendents was that Homeric epic was the product of a long tradition of oral story-telling, whereas the so-called "literary" epics of Virgil, Milton, and Blake, for example, though modeled upon the oral-derived poetry of ancient Greece, took a predominantly literary form. It was only late in the evolution of this tradition of European letters, with the discovery by Western scholars of the literature of other lands, that the designation of epic in its traditional oral sense, once nearly monopolized by the *Iliad* and the *Odyssey*, was extended to include the oral-derived narratives of Sumeria, India, Africa, Ireland, Japan, and other ancient cultures.

In repeating this important distinction between oral and literary epics, we must be careful, however, not to perpetuate the misleading notion, sometimes suggested in earlier writing on epic, that these modes of story-telling represent two air-tight, mutually exclusive, cultural categories.[6] The literary and cultural significance of the differences between traditions of oral and written transmission cannot be over-emphasized, but in many, perhaps most, traditions these forms of story-telling do not develop in total isolation from one another. Although efforts to record in writing stories traditionally passed on exclusively by word of mouth may in some cases spell the end of the epic oral tradition—as was eventually the case with the recording of Homeric epic in the sixth century B.C.E.—elsewhere the traditions of oral story-telling continue to thrive on a popular level, apparently oblivious to the possibly immobilizing effects of the written word. Nowhere is the cross-fertilization of the oral and the written more dramatic than in contemporary India where traditions of oral recitation, theater, and popular story-telling of the *Ramayana* story co-exist with an ongoing literary tradition, notwithstanding the existence of the two-thousand-year-old canonical account of Valmiki. In such ways, written and oral traditions may often evolve side by side, shaping each other throughout their on-going development. Just as the habits and conventions of oral story-telling may continue for centuries to exert important pressures on written accounts, so also previous recorded versions may serve as catalysts for popular revision and recreation. For these reasons, it is probably best to conceive of the oral and written modes not as sharply distinguished historical categories but as phases along an ever-present continuum between the oral and the written.[7] Although each of the texts considered here no doubt represents quite a distinct genealogy in its historical movement from oral to written tradition—and in the case of the David story this transition may have been quite negligible—as oral-derived texts, they are all situated somewhere in the midst of a general movement from oral to written modes of representation.

In view of the classical origins of Western conceptions of epic, it should come as no surprise then that none of the works presented here conform precisely to conventional Western profiles of the epic genre, except of course for the *Odyssey*, in reference to which, as we have seen, the genre was conceived in the first place. In the strictest sense of the term, therefore, we may find something slightly anachronistic and misleading in identifying even the cycle of stories associated with King Gilgamesh as epic. As John Maier suggests in his essay, the various stories associated with Gilgamesh were in all likelihood pieced together as one unified story rather late in their development and the earliest form of the story may well have been closer to what we might call wisdom literature than heroic poetry. Thus, although the Gilgamesh traditions are certainly the oldest accounts represented here, their appropriation as "epic" in the sense in which that term was traditionally used in the West has been recent and partly a matter of literary short-hand. For its part, the *Ramayana* poses a more serious challenge. Here we encounter a text situated in a literary tradition every bit as developed as that of ancient and classical Greece. Literary historians of the West have been accustomed for some time to refer to the *Ramayana* and the even more extensive narrative poem, the *Mahabharata*, as the two great Sanskrit epics. But until recently, the South Asian literary tradition was never beholden to Western theories about genre for conceptualizing its own literature, and according to the Indian system of classification, the *Mahabharata* is the chief representative of what is known in the Sanskrit tradition as *itihasa*, a term which might be rendered as something like "chronicle," while the *Ramayana*, was generally characterized as *adikavya*, the first or foundational poetic work.[8] In other words, from an Indian standpoint, the two Sanskrit "epics" are not to be construed as two alternative examples of a single generic form on the model of the *Iliad* and the *Odyssey*, the way they often have been in the Western literary world. Their origins, form of composition, and style of narration may well reflect two different traditions of story-telling in South Asia and perhaps even two different forms of literature. Thus, the mere existence of alternative theories of literature indigenous to these other traditions has the effect of relativizing the Western-derived term.

Yet putting aside all such preliminary disclaimers and caveats, in the pages to follow we will quickly see how much there is to be gained by considering these several ancient narratives collectively, as parts of a composite human whole. Although each bears the marks of its unique literary and cultural heritage, parallels of plot, theme, characterization, episode, and literary form cannot be avoided. As we will see in a moment, there are good historical reasons for believing that some of these parallels were by no means a matter of coincidence: none of these peoples, even when they lived on the ends of the then-known world, existed in a cultural or historical vacuum. But whatever the details of particular historical contacts or borrowing, the resemblance between these stories is often remarkable. Viewing them synoptically, one ranged among the others, yields glimpses into periods of human history that would remain otherwise forever inaccessible. All are set in a time of historical beginnings, when acts of bravery, violence, and conquest proved instrumental in the formation of a people and the shaping of a nation. All recount the exploits of a hero or heroes whose triumphs—and failings—prove to have a decisive impact on the destiny of an age and a culture. All reflect an entrenched culture of warriors and kings, whose acts of heroism and prowess on the battlefield become the subjects of song and celebration for a people just beginning to take stock of their historical, cultural, and religious heritage. And all of these stories, retold first by bards and the warriors themselves, came to serve as the basis for an ethnic and national tradition of history, religion, and literature documenting, sometimes encyclopedically, the crucially formative events of a people's early collective experience. This is the common literary and cultural ground shared by these stories, and it is on this basis of setting, story, and circumstance that we consider all of these ancient narratives under the heading of the epic voice.

Ancient Epic—A Narrative Web

While each of the five epics considered in this volume is addressed individually on its own terms and within its own literary and cultural context, their clustered configuration in this volume was not conceived at random. Indeed, a sequential study of the five will inevitably invite and provoke comparative questions and discussions of similar or parallel images, episodes, cultural values, narrative strategies, and poetic forms. Such discussions raise further questions of their own regarding possible historical connections between these epics and the cultures they embody and represent. Clearly, this is a vast and elusive topic, but it is also a valid and pressing one; so some brief suggestions seem called for. Nothing undertaken here can hope to be persuasive, much less conclusive. Our intent is merely to suggest the larger cultural and geographical context in which these several traditions arose. We begin with an assumption, concisely expressed by Sheldon Pollock when he wrote that "all literary cultures participate in what turn out to be networks, ultimately globalized networks, of borrowing, appropriating, reacting, imitating, emulating, rivaling...."[9] The question here is whether some or all of these five far-flung ancient works—*The Epic of Gilgamesh, The David Story, The Odyssey* of Homer, *The Ramayana,* and *The Táin*—may be thought to share a common "network." In suggesting that indeed there may be multiple connecting fibers reaching from one poem to another and perhaps entangling them all, we will arrange our brief comments under a series of comparative headings:

Prehistoric Substratum

Sir John Marshall, who directed the early British excavations in the Indus Valley, may have been the first but was far from the last to suggest "a tangible concrete connection between the religions of the Indus Valley and that of Mesopotamia."[10] Noting the remarkable resemblance between the figure of Enkidu and a similar Indus Valley type, Marshall concluded that "either the Indus Valley type must have been borrowed from Mesopotamia or the Mesopotamian from the Indian."[11] He himself came down in favor of the borrowing having been done by India in this instance. The far more sweeping conjecture to emerge from Marshall's work in Sind, however, was that the Indus Valley civilization of the third and second millennia B.C.E. was only part of a more vastly encompassing Chalcolithic civilization extending from the East Mediterranean to northern India. In sum, he argued that "if the Aryans were able to disseminate their religious ideas over half of Europe and Asia, there is no intrinsic reason why the older races who preceded them should not have done the same."[12] If anything like this were true, it would mean that at their deepest roots all of the epic traditions included in this volume would share some common cultural soil. But holding that larger thesis aside, both during and after the Sumerian and the Harrapan periods, trade can be documented between Mesopotamia and northern India, by sea via the Persian Gulf and by land across the Iranian Plateau.

MESOPOTAMIA AND ISRAEL

From Abraham's elusive origins in Ur and Haran to the legendary Hebrew sojourn in Egypt to its Exile in Babylon, i.e., for a period well over a thousand years, there is no denying the intimate historical and cultural connections between Israel and its neighbors. It is well established, for example, that decisive sections of Genesis—notably the Priestly Account of Creation and nearly the whole of the Flood Story—are dependent on Mesopotamian sources. In fact, large portions of the Hebrew Bible were likely composed or compiled either during or after Israel's forced deportation to the banks of the Euphrates. Indeed, the world of ancient Israel was hardly confined to its own borders. As Cyrus Gordon and Gary Rendsburg have argued, "in its thousand-year history in antiquity, Israel's contacts stretched from the Mediterranean coastal regions in the west to the Iranian (and perhaps Indian) lands in the east... Indeed, the great prophet Isaiah writing in the eighth century B.C.E. already recognized that Israel was part of a larger world that stretched to Egypt and beyond in one direction and to Mesopotamia (or Assyria, as he called it) and beyond in the other."[13] Furthermore, the well-known trade connections between Israel and South Arabia during the reign of Solomon continued for centuries and likely extended, either directly or indirectly, to India.

GREECE AND ISRAEL

In discussing the influence of Near Eastern myth on early Greek literature, specifically Hesiod, Homer's contemporary, the eminent classicist M.L. West points out that "what most strikes the modern traveler to Greece is that the country belongs not to Europe, but to Asia...in a certain measure it has always been so...." And he concludes, "As it was, the great civilizations lay in the East, and from the first, Greece's face was turned towards the sun. Greece is part of Asia; Greek literature is Near Eastern Literature."[14] This means that Israel and Greece drank for centuries from the same well. Indeed, the Mycenaeans had colonies, or at least trading posts, in Syria, Palestine, and Cyprus; and they surely formed a substantial contingent of the Sea Peoples who wrought havoc on the Levant at the close of the Bronze Age. It is even likely that the warriors who laid siege to Troy were cousins to the Philistines against whom Saul and David fought for the control of Palestine.

GREECE AND INDIA

Following from M.L. West's claim that from the start Greece faced East, the question then becomes "How far East?" Indo-European scholars such as Georges Dumézil and Émil Benveniste trace the linguistic and cultural roots of Greece and India to a common proto-Indo-European source. The Mycenaean and Rig Vedic civilizations were roughly contemporaneous and, for all their differences, developed closely cognate languages and cultures. Following their development, we can detect intriguing echoes of Vedic literature in the writings, for example, of Homer, Pythagoras, Herodotus, and Plato. Despite the vast spaces stretching between them, Greeks and Indians were hardly strangers to each other. Xerxes brought Indian warriors to Greece in 480 B.C.E., and Alexander brought Greek warriors to India in 327 B.C.E. Unlike the Indian invaders in Greece, the Greek invaders in India stayed on, founding provincial governments as they themselves assimilated into the population. But not all contacts between Greeks and Indians were hostile. Trade, diplomacy, art, and religion surely also played a role. For example, there is explicit textual evidence of Buddhist proselytizing in Greece during the reign of Ashoka (274–236 B.C.E.).[15] Furthermore, the Greek influence on Indian sculpture is well established, and a persuasive case can be made for limited Greek influence on classical Indian drama. Finally, closer to the concerns of this book, Wendy Doniger, in her recent and brilliant comparative study of Greek and Indian myth, argues that "texts from Greece and India share a large percentage of related cultural restraints (beginning with language)..." and concludes, in short, that the ancient Greeks and Indians are best seen as "cousins."[16]

IRELAND AND INDIA

Convinced of what he called "the archaism of Irish tradition," Myles Dillon, one of the preeminent Celtic scholars of the twentieth century and also a noted Sanskritist and Vedic scholar, demonstrated that "Ireland, on the margin of the Indo-European area, has preserved Indo-European characteristics that have been lost in most other regions of the West."[17] More specifically, he argued for a common tradition of court poetry, shared by India and Ireland, dating to the first millennium B.C.E. and, more broadly, suggested that "India and Ireland have preserved common Indo-European traditions in social organization, and in language and literature."[18] These same conclusions are widely supported by other Indo-European comparativists. One of these, Alf Hiltebeitel, in his analysis of the culminating duels of *The Táin* and *The Mahabharata*, i.e. the duel between Cú Chulainn and Fer Diad, on the one hand, and between Arjuna and Karna, on the other, after noting and considering the startling number of specific convergences between these two episodes, concluded that "we are dealing with related tales... (and) it is not unreasonable to propose that the two traditions (Irish and Indian) have each preserved and further developed on their own an archaic epic theme."[19]

IRELAND, GREECE, AND ISRAEL

The possibility, even likelihood, of biblical and classical influence on the *Táin* has been long acknowledged and argued by scholars of the *Táin*, since, in its surviving recensions, it is at least in part the creation of learned medieval scholars, most probably monks, steeped in and committed to the Bible and the classical tradition. For example, it has been suggested that, in the *Táin*, the character of Medb may have been modeled in part on the biblical Delilah and, more evidently, that Achilles may have served as one paradigm for the final shaping and enhancement of the central hero Cú Chulainn.[20]

CONCLUDING COMMENTS

That there was a web of historical connections, direct and indirect, linking the varied cultures from which the epics highlighted in this volume sprung is widely acknowledged. What corresponding connections we find or suspect among those epics is a much more complex and contested matter. As we are dealing here with stories, however, it is well to remember that no one travels lighter than a story-teller and few strangers are more welcome. Immaterial trade—stories, myths, and ideas—can and likely does go wherever material trade goes. In fact, we might conjecture that the former often finds its way to places the latter does not. In cultures wherein literacy was rare, books even rarer, mass-media non-existent, and entertainments few, hunger for and delight in stories must have been common and intense. Furthermore, anyone—merchants, warriors, slaves, sailors, priests, physicians, explorers, and kings—could be a story-teller or a listener, and probably was. Stories add no weight to anyone's load. Pots and merchants' seals wind up along established trade routes, whereas stories may be carried far off-track, like seeds carried by the wind. There is simply much we will never know and even more we can never prove about the lives of the world's most ancient and enduring narratives.

ACKNOWLEDGEMENTS

From its inception in the fall of 1999 till its present culmination, the academic program that gave rise to this book has been a collaborative undertaking. The editors would like to express our appreciation to the Humanities faculty of Hampshire College for their ongoing interest in our endeavor, and particularly to our former Dean, Mary Russo, for her enabling material and moral support throughout all phases of the project. For additional encouragement and support, we are indebted to the Hampshire College Center for the Book, Five Colleges Incorporated, Hampshire's Dean of Faculty Aaron Berman, and our president Gregory Prince. In addition, we would like to express our thanks to Christine McCarthy of the Hampshire College Bookstore for hosting our receptions and to our indefatigable student assistant Chris Braak for his invaluable technical support and overall assistance in helping us prepare for our biweekly lecture series. Finally, we would like to record our special appreciation to the various members of the inaugural class of the Hampshire Studies in the Humanities—Geoff Barstow, Chris Braak, Laura Fix, Kate Frederic, Justin Goldstein, Aaron Jorgensen, Matthew Latkiewicz, Joe Laycock, Erica Lewis, Dan McNamara, Nick Moen, Adrienne Perry, Christian Phillips, Prema Prabhakar, Erin Snyder, and Catharine Bell Wetteroth—whose insight, enthusiasm, and conscientiousness helped to make our program the memorable intellectual adventure that it was. It is to them that this first book of our series is dedicated.

ALAN D. HODDER & ROBERT E. MEAGHER
Hampshire College

NOTES

1. In Hans Jonas, "Change and Permanence: On the Possibility of Understanding History" *Social Research*, Autumn 1971, vol. 38, no. 3, p. 526.

2. Augustine, *Confessions*, X.17, Loeb Classical Library no. 27 (Cambridge, Mass.: Harvard University Press, 1970). Translation mine.

3. Normandi Ellis, trans., *Awakening Osiris: A New Translation of the Egyptian Book of the Dead* (Ann Arbor, Mich.: Phanes Press, 1988), p. 10.

4. Publius Terentius Afer, *Heauton Timorumenos*, 1.25, Loeb Classical Library no. 22 (Cambridge, Mass.: Harvard University Press, 1912). Translation mine.

5. In the *Republic*, for example, Plato invokes the plural form of the term to distinguish Homeric poetry from lyric poetry. See *Republic* 379a. Cf. Edith Hamilton and Huntington Cairns, eds., *Plato: The Collected Dialogues* (Princeton: Princeton University Press, 1961), p. 625. For the most fully developed theory of literature from the classical period, see Leon Golden

and O. B. Hardison, Jr., *Aristotle's Poetics: A Translation and Commentary for Students of Literature* (Englewood Cliffs, N.J.: Prentice-Hall, 1968).

6. For the classic treatment of the oral-formulaic theory, see Albert Lord, *The Singer of Tales* (Cambridge: Harvard University Press, 1960), and also his posthumously published, *The Singer Resumes the Tale* (Ithaca: Cornell University Press, 1995). John Miles Foley provides a critical assessment of the Parry-Lord theory in *The Theory of Oral Composition: History and Methodology* (Bloomington: Indiana University Press, 1988).

7. See John Miles Foley, *The Singer of Tales in Performance* (Bloomington: Indiana University Press, 1995). Also see Mark C. Amodio, "Contemporary Critical Approaches and Studies in Oral Tradition," in *Teaching Oral Traditions*, ed. John Miles Foley (New York: Modern Language Association, 1998), pp. 96–97.

8. See John Brockington, *The Sanskrit Epics* (Leiden: Brill, 1998).

9. Sheldon Pollock, "Literary History, Region, and Nation in South Asia," *Social Scientist* 23 (1995): 136.

10. Sir John Marshall, *Mohenjo-Daro and the Indus Civilization* (London: Arthur Probsthain, 1931), p. 58.

11. Ibid., p. 76.

12. Ibid., p. 58.

13. Cyrus H. Gordon and Gary A. Rendsburg, *The Bible and the Ancient Near East* (New York: W.W. Norton, 1997), p. 32. In this context, it is interesting to refer directly to the words of Isaiah 19:24–25: "In that day, Israel shall be a third partner with Egypt and Assyria as a blessing on earth; for the LORD of Hosts will bless them, saying, 'Blessed be My people Egypt, My handiwork Assyria, and My very own Israel.'" (New JPS Translation)

14. Hesiod, *Theogony*, edited with prolegomena and commentary by M.L. West (Oxford: Clarendon Press, 1966), pp. 30–31.

15. See Vincent A. Smith, *Asoka, the Buddhist Emperor of India* (Oxford: Oxford University Press, 1901), Rock Edict XIII, pp. 131–132.

16. Wendy Doniger, *Splitting the Difference: Gender and Myth in Ancient Greece and India* (Chicago: University of Chicago Press, 1999), p. 6.

17. Myles Dillon, "The Archaism of Irish Tradition," The Sir John Rhys Memorial Lecture, *Proceedings of the British Academy*, vol. xxxiii, 1947, p. 2.

18. Ibid., p. 20. See also Myles Dillon, *Celts and Aryans* (Simla: Indian Institute of Advanced Study, 1975), p. 146.

19. Alf Hiltebeitel, "Brothers, Friends, and Charioteers: Parallel Episodes in the Irish and Indian Epics," in *Homage to Georges Dumézil*, ed. Edgar C. Polomé, Journal of Indo-European Studies Monograph No. 3 (Washington: Institute for the Study of Man, 1982), pp. 104–105.

20. See Patricia Kelling, "The Táin as Literature," in *Aspects of the Táin*, ed. J.P. Mallory (Belfast: December Publications, 1992), pp. 69–95.

GILGAMESH

We begin our study of five ancient texts with what is arguably the oldest recorded extended narrative of human history—the ancient Sumerian story of Gilgamesh. Here we are presented with the traditional story of the king known as Gilgamesh, who ruled the ancient walled city of Uruk, located in an area of what is now southern Iraq, sometime in the Second Early Dynastic Period (ca. 2700-2500 B.C.E.). Retooled and refashioned by various scribal schools over a period of some 2000 years, the story, as we have it, was recorded in cuneiform by an otherwise unknown poet named Sîn-leqi-unninnī in the Akkadian language and preserved on twelve clay tablets that were later deposited in the library of Ashurbanipal in the ancient Assyrian city of Ninevah. Despite its extreme antiquity, the narrative turns on a familiar and well-nigh universal theme—the human quest for immortality. Indelibly, these ancient tablets sketch the turbulent career of King Gilgamesh, including the memorable story of the humanization of the primitive animal-man Enkidu; Enkidu's conflict with Gilgamesh and the subsequent cementing of their friendship; the killing of Humbaba, guardian of the cedar-grove; Gilgamesh's repudiation of the goddess Ishtar and resulting conflict with the Bull of Heaven; Ishtar's curse against Enkidu and his tragic death; and finally, Gilgamesh's pilgrimage to the ends of the earth to obtain the secret of immortality by which he hopes to ransom his beloved friend from the land of the dead. Included in the story of Gilgamesh's quest is an ancient version of the Flood story that predates the biblical story by a thousand years or more. For many centuries the central work of the Sumero-Akkadian literary tradition, the story of Gilgamesh has now taken its place as a foundational text in world literature. In the following essay, John Maier draws on a lifetime of work as a translator of *Gilgamesh* and expert Sumerologist in elucidating the structure and focus of the Gilgamesh story.

GILGAMESH TIMELINE

3800		Beginning of Uruk Period
3000		Emergence of early Sumerian cities
3000		Earliest Sumerian tablets
2800		Gilgamesh, king of Uruk
2600		Early Sumerian literature
2600–2400		Deification and worship of Gilgamesh
2350		Fall of Sumer
2200		Oral Gilgamesh poems
2100		Sumerian epics
2100–2000		Sumerian revival
2000		Oldest copy of *Gilgamesh* poem
1700		Old Babylonian Version of *Gilgamesh*
1500		Middle Babylonia Version of *Gilgamesh*
1200		Standard Version of *Gilgamesh*
800–200		Copies of *Gilgamesh* epic [Nineveh, Uruk, Babylon]
	B.C.E.	
19c	C.E.	Rediscovery of ancient Mesopotamia and decipherment of cuneiform

ANCIENT SUMER

GILGAMESH OF URUK

PROLOGUE

To the Orientalist, the story is a familiar one, the scene crowded with characters we feel we have seen before in literature. A great hero from Mesopotamia defeats the Elamites and is crowned king. The hero, Izdubar, is visited by the goddess of love herself. She provides him with enigmatic dreams, the most important of which is too difficult for his advisors to interpret. A call goes out to an ancient poet-seer, a lover of the natural world and solitude, a turbaned mystic who had separated himself voluntarily from humankind. Enticed to return to the city, Heabani interprets the dream.

There is more, of course, to the story. One episode describes "The Annual Sale of the Maidens of Babylon." Another describes "Ishtar's Descent to Hades," together with the escape of Tammuz from the world of the dead. When the poet-seer is killed fighting a god of death in the form of a dragon, his friend Izdubar sets out on an immense journey. He becomes immortal. He falls in love with a woman in the "World of Blessedness."

The story sounds more like the *1001 Nights* than *Gilgamesh*. Thanks to the hard work of an author who lived not far from here, in nearby Newtonville, the poem, *Ishtar and Izdubar, the Epic of Babylon* saw its way into print in 1884. The author was an attorney who practiced in Boston and earlier in San Francisco. He wrote a number of books, none better I think than *Ishtar and Izdubar, the Epic of Babylon*.

It is not, as you have no doubt guessed, very close to what we now think is *Gilgamesh*, or "The Epic of Gilgamesh," as many prefer. The odd thing is that the author, Leonidas Le Cenci Hamilton, had done his homework. He had read all that had been written about the tablets that had been discovered by George Smith in the early 1870s, and had put together a poem that seemed plausible, given the fragmentary nature of the cuneiform texts at that time.[1]

INTRODUCTION

There is little question that certain episodes in the Mesopotamian narrative *Gilgamesh* remained popular—and even gained popularity—through the nearly twenty five hundred years when Gilgamesh stories were written, copied, and profoundly revised. Even the Greeks seemed to have become interested in the stories of conflict, which pitted Gilgamesh and his friend Enkidu against extraordinary powers, the guardian of the forest Humbaba and the mighty Bull of Heaven that was sent to earth to teach the mortals a lesson. Besides a relatively large number of texts that have been excavated, some of them "school" texts used in the classroom to teach cuneiform writing, archaeologists have found many visual images, mainly cylinder seal impressions, that deal with the heroic acts of Gilgamesh and Enkidu. Because of the popularity of these episodes, scholars of our era like to identify the Standard Version of the stories by the Greek genre, "epic." And since epic poetry was, until the twentieth century of the Common Era, arguably the most important, certainly the most influential literary genre in the West, scholars automatically conferred upon the Gilgamesh stories the highest status not only within Mesopotamia but in the Western tradition as well. That is the reason the work is a "core" text in a seminar devoted to "The Epic Voice."

When nearly twenty years ago the late John Gardner and I translated the Akkadian text, we avoided calling it "The Epic of Gilgamesh," preferring to follow the colophons of the twelve tablets found at the Assyrian site of Nineveh, where it is referred to as the "series" *(iškaru) Gilgamesh*—even though John Gardner was preparing to teach the translation in a team-taught course at SUNY Binghamton on the epic tradition. Now that much more is known about the fragments of texts and the variants in the Gilgamesh tradition—about two-thirds of the original has now been recovered—I still prefer to think of it as something other than a traditional heroic narrative, something different, as the reading I propose will make clear.

Gilgamesh is certainly a collection of stories that were originally separate. I think we are still only beginning to see the brilliance of the synthesis that resulted. I approach the thorny question of the "unity" of *Gilgamesh* in a rather unusual way, by first considering features that seem difficult to fit into a unified work, and gradually letting the work unfold. Three elements—splitting, displacement and fronting—are prominent in this analysis.

The order of the large episodes that make up *Gilgamesh* is fairly easy to establish. Only the last, the notorious Twelfth Tablet, divides scholarly opinion as to its relevance to the narrative. After a Prologue, *Gilgamesh* turns to the Birth and Education of Enkidu; the long story of the campaign against Humbaba; Gilgamesh's rejection of the goddess Ishtar and the consequent conflict with the Bull of Heaven; Enkidu's death and funeral; and Gilgamesh's search for the meaning of life and death, which ends with the hero's return to his city, Uruk. Finally, in what I consider an epilogue, the story shifts to another view of Enkidu's death and a vision of the underworld.

It is true that the epic-like battles captured the imagination of the ancient world. But the agonizing journey of the distraught Gilgamesh who has lost his friend is reflected in a very different piece from the same collection of Nineveh texts that included *Gilgamesh*. A prophetess named Dunnaša-Amur of Arbela "identifies herself with Gilgamesh roaming the desert in search of eternal life, implying that ascetic denial of the body...played an important part in her own life."[2] The prophetess is inspired by Ishtar, and she seeks (and finds) not her own immortality but a better life for the king Assurbanipal (who collected texts from all over Assyria and the south).

> I roam the desert desiring your life. I cross over rivers and oceans. I traverse mountains and mountain chains. I cross over all rivers. Droughts and showers consume me and affect my beautiful figure. I am worn out, my body is exhausted for your sake.
>
> I have ordained life for you in the assembly of the all the gods. My arms are strong, they shall not forsake you before the gods. My shoulders are alert, they will keep carrying you.
>
> I keep demanding life for you with my lips.... (41)[3]

I must confess that it was the agonizing quest that first riveted my attention, as an undergraduate, to the text that has consumed so much of my adult life. So I was delighted to see that the mystical side of Gilgamesh caught the attention of an ancient reader as well.

"Noah's Wife" in Gilgamesh

Let us begin in an unlikely place, not at the beginning of the poem, but near the end of the quest for "life," which takes up the second half of the narrative. Consider one of the most obscure figures in *Gilgamesh*, whom I will call for convenience "Noah's Wife." She is of course not the wife of the biblical Noah, but the wife of the Noah-figure who is sought by Gilgamesh. If anyone has the answer to his questions about life and death it would be the great exception, variously named Utnapishtim, Utu-napishti, or Uta-napishti, a mortal who escapes the common lot of humanity and is raised to a god-like status for his help in preventing the utter annihilation of humankind. Because the flood story which the sage tells Gilgamesh was not originally part of the Gilgamesh story and develops a remarkable life of its own (beyond the book of Genesis), its appearance in *Gilgamesh* has long been considered problematic.

"Noah's wife" is all the more remarkable because different traditions portray her as one who carries *gnosis* to those enlightened ones who are able to understand it—and as one of only two women mentioned by name in the Qur'an as an archetypal betrayer of men.

Because she remains anonymous, Noah's wife is often ignored in readings of *Gilgamesh*. In sharp contrast to her garrulous husband, the wife at first glance seems to epitomize the marginalized, silenced females in Middle Eastern societies—evidence, perhaps, that the status of women diminished from Sumerian times through the second and first millennia B.C.E.

She does, in fact, have very little to say. But I think her presence and her few spoken lines are far more important than they first appear. Utnapishtim's wife appears in two of the six columns in Tablet XI. At the end of the flood story, she is raised, with her husband, to the special status that Gilgamesh may be seeking.

> "Enlil came up to the ark.
> He seized my hand and picked me up,
> And he raised my wife up, making her kneel at my side.
> He touched our foreheads and, standing between us, he blessed us.
> 'Before this, Utnapishtim has been human.
> Now Utnapishtim and his wife are transformed, being like us gods.
> Let Utnapishtim live far off, at the source of all rivers.'"
> (XI.[iv.]189–95)⁴

As in the Sumerian flood story—but quite unlike the biblical flood—the wife is given a prominent place and translated into a kind of divine state along with her husband, although she is given no specific role to play in rescuing humanity. Despite this prominence, she remains silent. Since the flood story is presented by Utnapishtim himself, and is clearly a story whose wisdom requires Gilgamesh's complete attention to understand, the storyteller may be following a long-held tradition in the Middle East, where men are advised not to discuss their wives with other men—nor even to mention their names.

No sooner does Gilgamesh hear the story but is given the Sleeping Test, which he fails miserably. If he cannot stay awake, how can he expect to live in this exalted status? Utnapishtim comes up with a clever way to convince Gilgamesh that he has been asleep for a week, as the wife fulfills a traditional role in baking bread each day. Easily overlooked is the very brief exchange between Utnapishtim and his wife when Gilgamesh falls asleep.

> Utnapishtim said to his wife,
> "Look at this hero who asks for life!
> Sleep has blown over him like a wet haze!"
>
> His wife answers Utnapishtim the remote:
> "Touch the man, so he'll wake up.
> He'll take the road, return in peace.
> He'll go out through the gate, returning to his land."

Utnapishtim says to her, his wife:
"A man who is trouble will give you trouble.
Come, bake bread for him, place it near him, by his head,
And the days he sleeps score on the wall."
(VI.[iv.]202–12)[5]

Here the wife offers her advice, a compassionate response to Gilgamesh's plight. Utnapishtim sees humans (*amelutu*), not men in particular, as bad (*ragagu*), so he rejects her advice and instead proposes a scheme that will convince Gilgamesh that he is unfit for divinity.

The wife comes to Gilgamesh's aid again in a rather peculiar turn to the story. Gilgamesh is crushed by his failure and once again sees only death before him. Utnapishtim closes off the possibility that other humans will make the journey to him by cursing the boatman. The best he can offer Gilgamesh is a purifying cleansing and a new robe—and a new role as elder in the city of Uruk. As column v ends, the two men board the boat and begin their return to Uruk.

The turn comes just at the beginning of column vi. The wife chides Utnapishtim for neglecting his time-honored role as host.

Then his wife said to him, to Utnapishtim the remote:
"Gilgamesh has come here—has strained, has toiled—
What have you given him as he returns to his land?"
(XI.[vi].258–60)[6]

Immediately Gilgamesh and the boatman turn about, and Utnapishtim this time follows her advice. The great irony at this point is that Gilgamesh returns only to receive what appears to be the greatest gift—a plant like a box-thorn, found deep in the waters, with which a man can renew his youth.

Gilgamesh finds—and loses—the magic herb. It is the last and, as it is the closest he comes to achieving the "life" he has sought, most bitter of the many disappointments he has suffered. He and the boatman return to Uruk, and Gilgamesh calls attention to what is his most conspicuous compensation, the walls of his city, and his role there as king.

The author of a children's illustrated series on Gilgamesh offers an intriguing spin on the loss of the plant. In *The Last Quest of Gilgamesh*, Ludmila Zeman depicts a serpent slithering down a tree and snatching the plant from a sleeping Gilgamesh.[7] The serpent and the tree suggest the biblical Garden of Eden. The explanation of the serpent's theft of the flower is, however, that it is Ishtar's revenge for having been rejected by Gilgamesh. (Gilgamesh mourns his loss, but is suddenly given back Enkidu—with the help of the woman who had seduced and humanized Enkidu at the beginning of the story.)

Gilgamesh XI does, of course, feature a snake *(seru, nešu ša qaqqari)* but no hint that Ishtar is behind the theft. Indeed, the return of Gilgamesh to Uruk, as I read the text, is a return to his role as *en* (roughly translated as "lord" or "priest-king") and a special relationship to Ishtar. But more on that later. But Ludmila Zeman's bold interpretation is useful in seeing the later episodes of *Gilgamesh* tied to earlier ones, particularly where the goddess Ishtar is concerned.

Siduri the Barmaid

Before drawing conclusions from the brief appearances of Utnapishtim's wife, it is important to consider another female who gives advice, this time to Gilgamesh directly. Tablet X opens with Gilgamesh at the "lip of the sea" where dwells Siduri, "the Barmaid" (*sabitu*). Andrew George, who refers to her as Shiduri, a "wise old goddess," prefers to call her a "tavern-keeper" (George, 75). Like many Mesopotamian terms, *sabitu* is difficult to translate into modern English. She owns a tavern that includes a brothel, usually, but it is difficult for us to see the cultic and sexual connection with dispensing wisdom, which she does in the text.[8] The house she keeps is often sacred, usually related to Ishtar and the "sacred marriage" between Ishtar and her lover Dumuzi. Prostitution, over which Ishtar ruled, was practiced there. And Siduri's name is sometimes—though not here—written with the divine determinative (*dingir*).

Siduri is one of several figures Gilgamesh meets along his difficult path.[9] Before Siduri, Gilgamesh was assisted by the half-human, half-scorpion couple, male and female, and perhaps another figure. After Siduri, Gilgamesh meets with Urshanabi the Boatman and then Utnapishtim. Siduri sees him coming and bars the door against him, worrying that he looks like a killer (*muna'iru*). He repeats his lament to her as to the others, and asks for directions to Utnapishtim. At first she discourages him.

> "Gilgamesh, there has never been a crossing,
> and none from the beginning of days has been able to cross the sea.
> None but Shamash crosses the sea; apart from Shamash, no one crosses.
> Painful is the crossing, troublesome the road,
> And everywhere the waters of death stream across its face."
> (X.[ii.]20–25)

Then, like Circe in *The Odyssey* (X.503–40), who provides Odysseus with advice on crossing the river of death to consult with the prophet, Siduri shows Gilgamesh the way.

"Even if you, Gilgamesh, cross the sea
when you arrive at the waters of death, what would you do?
There, Gilgamesh, lives Urshanabi, boatman to
   Utnapishtim.
The things of stone are with him.
In the heart of the forest he picks up the Urnu-snakes.
Show him your face.
If it is possible, cross with him.
If it is not possible, come back." (X.[ii.]26–331)[10]

While the references are still rather obscure, it is clear that Siduri enables Gilgamesh to complete the journey. The secret lore she gives him is often disappointing to modern scholars, who know that an earlier (Old Babylonian) version of the Gilgamesh stories has her give very different advice. Instead of chasing after immortality, Gilgamesh should enjoy ordinary life: a full belly, dancing and playing, fresh garments, clean living, and the child he holds on his knee—and the spouse who delights in him. That very practical advice is an important dimension to ancient "wisdom." *Gilgamesh*, however, seems rather to focus on a different sort of "wisdom," secrets of the gods and special bits of information for solving apparently insoluble problems.

An Elamite version of Gilgamesh's quest has Siduri (or Shiduri), clearly a divine being, as the *object* of the hero's search. He asks her to make it possible for him to give birth! Of course he is told that his request is impossible, but he is persuaded that life offers other things for him especially.[11] While the kind of wisdom Siduri dispenses differs from version to version, it is evident in the Standard Version of *Gilgamesh* that Siduri is but one of several important figures along the path. The central place she has in other versions gives way to Utnapishtim.

We can see in Utnapishtim's wife and Siduri a process that involves both splitting and displacement. Utnapishtim's wife is a vestige of a different, possibly earlier divine figure, surely a goddess who holds the key to life and is approached for her transformative powers (much like Enlil in the flood story). In all versions of Gilgamesh's quest, he is given not the "life" he seeks, but some compensation. In the earliest version that has been discovered so far, very close to the time of the historical Gilgamesh, the compensation appears to be leadership of the community—he is anointed with "first-quality oil"—rather than "a life of long days." In "The Early Dynastic Hymn to Gilgamesh," the hero carries off an "herb-pot of life." In a meadow the pot is set aside on the banks of a river—and presumably lost, as the plant in the Standard Version is lost. In that text it is not clear who is offering the "herb-pot of life" (*úgur-zi*) and the "tree"—or bush (*giš-ti*)—of life; it is one who is a "wise physician" (*a-su-géštu*).[12]

Instead of the central life-dispensing, "wisdom"-dispensing goddess, the Standard Version gives us Utnapishtim. His wisdom consists of the "secret" of the gods that is the scandal during which the most powerful of the gods, Enlil, and the mother goddess (significantly identified with Ishtar), learn through experience. The god Ea with the assistance of his mortal follower, Utnapishtim, foils the plan of the other gods. Utnapishtim tells the story directly to Gilgamesh in the manner of a good storyteller, prompting the listener to pay close attention to the wisdom the story contains.

Utnapishtim's story of the flood takes up almost two hundred lines of Tablet XI. The account of the flood shares so many details with the later biblical account that it is not surprising that this section of *Gilgamesh* created a sensation in the 1870s when George Smith found the tablets at Nineveh. Some lines are so close to the Bible that they provide the best parallel to biblical texts among the many cuneiform texts that have been discovered since then. The very prominence of the flood story in Tablet XI creates a problem for a unified reading of *Gilgamesh*. It seems clear—and the recently recovered Early Dynastic Gilgamesh hymn confirms—that the early versions of Gilgamesh do not contain the flood story or the sage Utnapishtim. The flood story itself is known from a fragmentary Sumerian text and several versions of *Atrahasis*, an Akkadian poem from the Old Babylonian period in which the flood is the last of three attempts by the gods to destroy humankind. In each attempt Ea and his man, known by the epithet *atra-hasis*, i.e., "exceedingly wise," find a way to thwart the powerful Enlil. In all versions of the story Enlil and Ea are finally reconciled. One way of looking at the story is to see that the powerful Enlil ultimately learns from his mistakes—and rewards the sage with his special status. *Gilgamesh* confirms what is nearly universal in Mesopotamian thought: that humans were created mortal; that some part of them will live on after death; but that such life in the underworld is difficult and tenuous at best—never a situation sought by humans.

Thus the story Utnapishtim tells Gilgamesh, even though it ends with the translation of Utnapishtim and his wife into a unique godlike status, offers Gilgamesh no hope for a similar transformation. "In your case, now," Utnapishtim asks, "who will assemble the gods for you so that the life you seek you may discover?" (XI.[iv.] 197–98). It is a rhetorical question, of course. Utnapishtim follows it with the challenge mentioned above: see if you can remain awake for a week. Gilgamesh immediately falls asleep for a week.

The flood story is so well integrated with other pieces of narrative related to Utnapishtim and his wife, and the whole is so well integrated with the Standard Version as a whole that it is difficult to think of *Gilgamesh* without it. Yet in displacing another, earlier version in which Gilgamesh travels a difficult course in search of life—even without a reference to Enkidu, by the way—the Standard Version retains certain vestiges of the other version. The wife of Utnapishtim is one such fragment of the powerful goddess who is eclipsed by Utnapishtim in this version. Siduri, split off and displaced, is another trace of that other story.

ISHTAR AND THE FLOOD

One of the most important questions debated by Assyriologists today is the status of women through the long event of Mesopotamian history. On one side are scholars like Tikva Frymer-Kensky who think that the goddesses of Sumer portray complex and important roles in society that mirror women's roles early, but that the goddesses themselves come to be marginalized, and with them, the status of women. Other scholars, like Rivka Harris, are not so sure that the status of women changed significantly from first to last, that is, from the fourth millennium B.C.E. through Hellenistic times.[13]

The great exception is the goddess of Uruk, Inanna, known in *Gilgamesh* in her Akkadian identity as Ishtar. Much has been made of Gilgamesh's brilliant rejection of Ishtar in Tablet VI, a story that like much of *Gilgamesh* has parallels in the older Sumerian poetry. In "Bilgames and the Bull of Heaven," Inanna offers gifts to the hero if he will be "her man," but it is the hero's *mother*, the wise Ninsun, who persuades him not to accept her offer—and for a most interesting reason: "The gifts of Inanna must not enter your chamber,/ the divine Palace Lady must not *weaken* (your) warrior's arm!" (George, 170). As in Tablet VI, the goddess is furious at the rejection and demands that the hero be punished. The Bull of Heaven is sent down. The heroes defeat the Bull of Heaven, and Enkidu, as he does in Tablet VI, cuts off a part of the body to throw at the goddess. The two humiliating gestures—Gilgamesh's refusal and Enkidu's crude taunting of the goddess—bring the great goddess as close to the level of humans as is to be found anywhere in Mesopotamian literature.

It is worth noting that the Sumerian "Bilgames and the Bull of Heaven" is dedicated to the great goddess, and that, as I read the final lines of Tablet XI, the wisdom of Gilgamesh's search for life involves a sober recognition of his duties as king of Uruk—and a reconciliation with the goddess of the city from whom he derives his authority.

> Gilgamesh said to him, to Urshanabi, the Boatman,
> "Go up, Urshanabi, onto the walls of Uruk.
> Inspect the base, view the brickwork.
> Is not the very core made of oven-fired brick?
> Did not the seven sages lay down its foundation?

> In [Uruk], house of Ishtar, one part is city,
> one part orchards, and one part claypits.
> Three parts including the claypits make up Uruk."
> (303–307)

Since all interpretations of a unified Standard Version depend on a reading of the final lines of Tablet XI, I offer also Andrew George's recent, rather different translation of the very last lines:

> A square mile is city, a square mile date-grove,
>   a square mile is clay-pit,
> half a square mile the temple of Ishtar:
>   three square miles and a half is Uruk's expanse.
> (George, 99)

The view of the city walls exactly repeats the opening of *Gilgamesh*—and has persuaded many critics that the view so frames the story that the next tablet, the notorious Tablet XII, should not be considered part of *Gilgamesh*. I will speak to that problem later. The last two lines of Tablet XI are also part of the frame and, I think, reinforce what all Mesopotamians knew, even if they had never seen Uruk, that the famous old city was centered in the temple of Ishtar.

There is a subtle change in the flood story that also speaks to the centrality of Ishtar in this poem. A motif in *Atrahasis* is found here. When the flood is let loose the destruction is so great that the gods themselves become frightened. The mother goddess then remembers that the humans who are dying everywhere are her children. She repents of her part in the decision to bring about the flood—and later wants to keep Enlil from enjoying the sacrifice that Utnapishtim makes when the waters recede.[14]

Twice in *Gilgamesh* XI the mother goddess is called *belet-ili*, Lady of the Gods. Only in *this* version of the story is the mother goddess identified as Ishtar. In the long history of Mesopotamian worship of Inanna/Ishtar, it is rare to see her portrayed as a mother. (The great exception is late, in the Neo-Assyrian period, the period of the Ninevite text of *Gilgamesh*.)

> Ishtar cried out like a woman giving birth,
> The sweet-voiced lady of the gods cried out,
> "The days of old are turned to clay
> since I spoke evil in the Assembly of the Gods.
> How could I speak evil in the Assembly of the Gods?
> How could I cry out for battle for the destruction of my
>   people?
> I myself gave birth to my people!
> [Now] like the children of fish they will fill the sea!"
> (XI.[iii].116–23)

> *i-šes-si ᵈIŠ.TAR ki-ma a-lit-ti*
> *ú-nam-ba ᵈbe-let—ilani ta-bat rig-ma*
> *mu-mu ul-tu-ú a-na ti-it-ti lu-ú i-tur-ma*
> *áš-šú a-na-ku ina pu-hur ilani aq-bu-ú lemuttu*
> *ki-i aq-bi ina pu-hur ilani lemuttu*
> *ana hul-lu-uq nišu-ia qab-la aq-bi-ma*
> *a-na-ku-ma-ma ul-la-da ni-šu-ú-a-a-ma*
> *ki-i maru nuni ú-ma-al-la-a tam-ta-am-ma*
> (after Parpola XI. 117–24)

Like the angry Enlil, Mother Ishtar *learns* in the process of destroying human life.¹⁵ Enlil is still angry when he learns that a human has escaped, but after a bitter confrontation with the wise Ea, is reconciled to the crafty god and to Utnapishtim, as we have seen. Before that reconciliation, the "lady of the gods" invites all the gods except Enlil to approach the offering Utnapishtim has given. She will never forget the devastation, and she chides Enlil for slaughtering her people without proper discussion in the assembly of the gods (XI.[iv.]162–69).¹⁶

As Utnapishtim tells the story to Gilgamesh, then, the high gods learn from what is seen as a terrible mistake. But what does Gilgamesh—or Utnapishtim, for that matter—learn?

GILGAMESH AND WISDOM

The flood story in *Gilgamesh* follows the precedent of Sumerian myths by opening *in medias res*, in the middle of things, without explaining the purpose of the story or the motivation of the characters. Such explanations, if they are made explicitly, come later, usually at the end of the story. (Since many cuneiform tablets are damaged at the beginning and end, the point of many tales is thus difficult to reconstruct.) Ishtar learns a lesson about the gods acting precipitously, without talking things out in the assembly—that is, about arbitrary and capricious rule. She learns this even before Ea makes the point explicit when he accuses Enlil in very similar terms. Utnapishtim begins his story with the decision of the gods, simply "The great gods stirred their hearts to make the Flood" (XI.[i.]14).

It is only later, after the story, when Utnapishtim is urged by his wife to show compassion to the visitor, that Utnapishtim provides what may be an explanation for the gods' anger toward humanity. Earlier I cited Utnapishtim's curious rationale for disregarding her advice: "A man who is trouble will give you trouble" (XI.[iv.]210). The line is a tricky one to deal with. Clearly it is a line that refers to the man who is sleeping in their midst, and we were reminded of

Gilgamesh's approach to Siduri, when she bolted the door before him, thinking him a killer. His terrible journey begins in the intense grief over Enkidu and includes not only profound grief but a turn to savagery and madness—rather like the *furor* that overtakes Herakles, in a motif that deeply influenced Western narratives. Tearing off the clothes that mark him as a city man and ruler, Gilgamesh takes on the skin of a lion and slaughters wild beasts in his relentless search for an answer to the problem of death.

What makes Utnapishtim's line difficult is that it seems to be cast in the form of a proverb. Andrew George translates it, "Man is deceitful, he will deceive you" (XI.219). In Akkadian it reads *rag-ga-at a-me-lu-tu i-rag-gi-ig-ki* (Parpola XI.218). The term *amelutu* does not refer to a man, either as male or as an individual; rather, it is *humanity* that is "deceitful." So Gilgamesh will be trouble because humans are trouble. In retrospect, Utnapishtim may, through dialogue with his wife, have hit upon the motive of the flood.

I rather like Andrew George's solution to the problem. Humans are deceitful and Gilgamesh will deceive the wife. Understood this way, the line looks back to the deceitfulness of the god Ea in subverting the gods' plan and the tricky speech he advises Utnapishtim to give to his fellow citizens (XI.[i.].36–47). Utnapishtim has to con his fellows into building the immense ark without actually telling them that they are about to be slain in the flood. The passage is a masterpiece of metaphorical deception. It exhibits better than any single passage in *Gilgamesh*—perhaps in Mesopotamian literature—the cunning nature of Ea and the "wisdom" that he was credited with throughout Mesopotamian history.

The verb used here, though, is problematic. The *Chicago Assyrian Dictionary* gives only a single instance of the verb *ragagu* (14/62) in all the cuneiform texts that have been excavated so far—this one. The *CAD* translates it, "mankind is wicked and will commit a wrong against you." *A Concise Dictionary of Akkadian* considers the verb "to be(come) mischievous" (295). Understanding the word involves comparing it with the Sumerian equivalent, *inim-níg-erím*, suggested by the ancients themselves, and other forms of the root, *rgg*. Adjectives, nouns, and participles, as with this verb form, follow the only form that is used extensively, *raggu* (*CAD* 14/67–69). What is striking about its use elsewhere—as wicked, evil, malicious, criminal, and wrongdoing that often has a suggestion of violence about it—is that *raggu* is often used with synonyms (*ajabu, senu*) and antonyms, "law-abiding" and the like. In other words, *raggu* is used most often as a generalized term—alas, not for deceptiveness—but for wrongdoing. Many of the gods, Marduk, Shamash, and Ishtar among them, are said to "hate" *raggu*. This would accord with the verb form used here with the abstraction, humanity. Although Utnapishtim and his wife were once (mere) humans, he now sees humans as, essentially, malicious.

That may then be the motive behind the flood, as Utnapishtim understands it. Characterizing "humanity," though, looks back to a very early episode in *Gilgamesh*, one that has occasioned a great deal of comment. It is an example of what I am calling "fronting," a literary device that is brilliantly employed in this poem, which in other ways may be seen as placing "bricks" of traditional narrative in some sort of order. We are only beginning to see the architectonics of the larger work.

The episode I am referring to has been discussed so frequently that I will simply mention it here: the birth and early life of Enkidu. Created at the request of citizens of Uruk, who are troubled by Gilgamesh's extravagances—if not wrongdoing—Enkidu grows in the wilderness and is so much a part of the wild life that he threatens the hunter who depends upon it. Gilgamesh knows what to do: send a temple woman into the wilderness to seduce Enkidu. The woman, one of whose titles is now read often as if it were a personal name, Shamhatu, is one of those figures in Mesopotamian religious life that is virtually impossible to understand in our Western Judeo-Christian categories. Her very explicit sexual encounter with Enkidu illustrates Shamhatu's connection with the raw and often dangerous sexuality attributed to Ishtar. She is also among the mourners for Enkidu. Regularly seen as a "sacred prostitute," the *harimtu* is one of a group of cultic officiants Richard A. Henshaw prefers to see as those who "interpret fertility and sexuality."[17]

I must pass over, reluctantly, Shamhatu's praise of Enkidu's godlike "wisdom" after the long sexual act that alienates Enkidu from the animals in the wild. She praises, rather, his godlike beauty (George I.107). And Tablet II, in which Shamhatu leads Enkidu to the life of animal husbandry and teaches him to drink beer and eat bread, the products of agriculture, is still in a very fragmentary condition. It is regularly filled out with lines from Old Babylonian Gilgamesh texts. Where Old Babylonian and later versions exist, the *contrasts* between them turn out to be as important as the similarities. But the larger shape of the episode seems clear enough. Shamhatu cares for Enkidu almost as a mother would. He sits at her feet when she describes Uruk and Gilgamesh. She brings him through what Jacques Lacan has called the Mirror Stage into the Symbolic. Once Enkidu is able to speak, he is able to learn from Shamhatu and the shepherds and is prepared to enter the city.[18] Gilgamesh already is the city-man par excellence and is praised greatly—although his practices as king evoked protests. He will be chided by the elders, too, as a young man, too anxious to make a name for himself to heed the danger of challenging Humbaba.

Both Enkidu, the *lullu*, or primal human, and the "civilized" Gilgamesh have much to learn, then, and two women provide the men with what they need to be human. Ninsun, the wise goddess who is the mother of Gilgamesh, is an interpreter of dreams and one who offers wise counsel. Shamhatu raises Enkidu to appreciate the full life of the city. Later, when Enkidu is dying, he curses the woman who has made him human, but no less than the high god Shamash persuades him that Shamhatu has given him the essentials of a full life. He blesses her.

Both Ninsun and Shamhatu dispense wisdom to the men. Then, like Siduri and Utnapishtim's wife, they largely disappear from view. As has been noticed before, the females in the story largely function as role-players; when they have discharged their functions, they are no longer needed. The Standard Version of *Gilgamesh* brilliantly overlays two stories of the development of humankind—at least of men. The birth and death of Gilgamesh are ignored in the story, though we now know that both were of interest from Sumerian times. Rather we have the complete life of Enkidu, including his new life in the underworld. The focus with Gilgamesh is different: the achieving of a "name," through heroic deeds and his search for life. In the process he must learn what it is to be a king.

Sumerian stories associated Gilgamesh with the goddess of wisdom, Nisaba, and with Enki/Ea, the god who, as we have seen, through deception saved humanity from the flood. The Sumerian versions of the conflict with Humbaba, "Bilgames and Huwawa," are dedicated to the goddess and turn on a solution provided by Enki.[19] "The Death of Bilgames" resolves the problem of Gilgamesh's curious combination of human and divine—he is only "two-thirds god" and therefore subject to death—by assigning "governorship of the Netherworld" as his fate; "his god, Enki" shows him a place where his problem can be solved (George 203, 205).

Ea, though prominent in the flood story in the Standard Version of *Gilgamesh*, as we have seen, has a diminished role generally. The god who is increasingly important is another one associated with knowledge and judgment, the sun god, Utu/Shamash. I have argued elsewhere that Mesopotamian literature shows two quite different notions of "wisdom," and that the distinction between them is clear in the Standard Version of *Gilgamesh* (275–304).[20] One form deals with the ordinary workings of the universe, often shrewd common sense observations such as one sees in proverb collections, and related to matters of justice; the other is trickier, mostly problem-solving that requires unusual responses to apparently unresolvable conflicts, and is related to the ambiguities of language itself.[21]

A Late Babylonian text of *Gilgamesh* found in his city of Uruk connects the two gods in a most interesting way. Gilgamesh's mother asks Shamash if her son's fate is not to that he will share the heavens with the sun and the moon, "grow wise with Ea" in the Apsû—and on earth will rule Mesopotamia with the help of the goddess Irnina. Ninsun also knows that his ultimate fate is to dwell in the underworld.[22]

The text from Uruk fits the context in Tablet III of our poem, which has Ninsun climbing steps to a roof[23] where she offers a smoke offering to Shamash—a scene that has a remarkable parallel in *The Odyssey* where it is Penelope who makes the offering.[24] On the roof Ninsun asks the question that I think is critical to a reading of *Gilgamesh*, and it is significant that it is Shamash who is addressed: "Why have you raised up my son Gilgamesh and laid on him a restless heart that will not sleep?" (III.ii.10; George, 24). Shamash does not answer the question at this point. After the long address to Shamash, Ninsun descends and adopts Enkidu by placing him among the "votaries of Gilgamesh,/ the priestesses, the hierodules and the women of the temple" (George, 27). Shamash guides the men into the forest, where they defeat Humbaba. The answer to Ninsun's question, if it is answered at all, comes much later, when Shamash reconciles Enkidu to his fate, a mortal who has enjoyed, thanks to Shamhatu, the best that human life offers (VII.iii.33–51).

Still, Enkidu is terrified of the underworld. If there is a single thread that runs through Mesopotamian thought, it is that humans are fated to work for the gods and then to die. Depictions of the underworld are uniformly dark and unhealthy. Tablet XII will complete the picture begun in Tablet VII. For now it is enough to emphasize that Enkidu, though his birth and death are rather unusual, proceeds through the life cycle of humans, and ends where no human wishes to go. The Uruk text of Tablet III suggests that Ninsun already knows the fate in store for her son: with all of his associations with the gods (above, on the earth, and below), he will yet die—but will have a privileged place as judge in the underworld.

In our poem, gods and humans alike must learn—from experience, guided through the process by the wise figures, especially Ea, Shamash, and Ninsun. I have argued that a reading of the poem that connects episodes that were either very different or completely absent from earlier versions of Gilgamesh stories enables us to add Siduri, Utnapishtim's wife, and the prostitute Shamhatu to the list. The goddesses and humans who assist Enkidu and Gilgamesh along the way do, largely, disappear from view once their role is fulfilled. And as I read the Standard Version, our poem does transform an earlier motif, where Gilgamesh made his agonizing way to the great goddess, dispenser of advice and life-giving herbs, into one that replaces the goddess with the mortal who has been deified, Utnapishtim. In the process, vestiges of the great goddess are displaced, from Utnapishtim's wife backwards to Siduri and Shamhatu.

If this means a marginalization of the goddess and perhaps of women as well, I would argue that the vestiges of the great goddess are recombined on another level, as aspects of Ishtar. Simo Parpola has argued that Assyrian thinkers turned Sumero-Babylonian theology in a striking way in the direction of monotheism. The national god Assur, he claims, was a transcendent figure, about which there is little of myth or artistic representation. The many gods of Mesopotamia came to be seen as aspects of the transcendent Assur.[25] Of the many aspects of Assur, Ishtar is the most important; she is the "word" of Assur through whom the prophets learn the will of god. The transcendence of Assur then, in Neo-Assyrian times, was quite compatible with the exaltation of Ishtar, which we know was also a prominent feature of the period in which our version of *Gilgamesh* was written.[26]

Some of the aspects of Ishtar have been recognized for many years. Figures that involve love, especially sexual activity, and war were long attached to Inanna/Ishtar. The wisdom aspect is less obvious, and the motherly concern for, especially, the Assyrian kings, becomes prominent in the later periods. Those two aspects are, as I have suggested, combined in Ishtar's recognition of and her repentance for her role in the flood.

In the central episode of *Gilgamesh* the hero rejects Ishtar (Tablet VI.i-ii) in lines so clever and eloquent that they are often taken as the final wisdom of the poem. Ishtar is chided for her inconstancy, but more pointedly, she is exposed for the way in which she has changed the fates of all her lovers, beginning with the famous Dumuzi/Tammuz.[27] Her response to Gilgamesh is anything but eloquent. In the Sumerian parallel to this episode, in fact, the goddess not only flies upward to her father's heaven—another parallel to the Homeric epics noted by Walter Burkert—but gets her way, sending the Bull of Heaven to take her vengeance upon Gilgamesh and Enkidu, by screaming so loud that her father gives in to her demands.[28]

The insults Gilgamesh hurls at Ishtar is paralleled by Enkidu's demeaning gesture of flinging a part of the slain Bull of Heaven at the goddess. These two acts, by mortals, bring the Mesopotamian gods to their lowest level in Mesopotamian literature. But just as Enkidu repents his cursing of Ishtar's Shamhatu, Gilgamesh moves though a succession of Ishtar's avatars to a reconciliation with Ishtar that comes when he realizes his proper role as king.

The final lines of Tablet XI do not state it explicitly, but they present an enlightened hero, willing to share the plant of rejuvenation with the elders of his city and returning to Ishtar's city, by implication returning to the goddess herself. Gilgamesh is *šarru,* or king, of Uruk, a rank the Sumerians called *lugal,* the "big man." In returning to Ishtar, though, he is returning to an earlier, pre-*lugal,* understanding of kingship. Judging from the many cylinder seal impressions from Archaic Uruk of the fourth millennium—and other visual representations like the famous Uruk Vase—the figure known in Uruk as the *en,* inadequately translated as "lord" or interpreted as "priest-king," combined the functions of king with the role of spouse selected by the great goddess of the city.[29] In addition to showing the *en* hunting lions and bulls, and in one instance using his bow against humans, and acting as judge, Mesopotamian art depicted him as a "good shepherd," feeding his flocks; anointing another person; and more frequently, bringing gifts, including sacrifices, to the temple. The temple is marked by symbols of Inanna, and the *en* was the lover selected by her.[30]

Once Gilgamesh has gained wisdom—what it is to be human and what it is to be king—he returns to his role as spouse of Ishtar.

THE EPILOGUE: A WISE GILGAMESH

Of the many risks John Gardner and I took in our 1984 translation of *Gilgamesh,* some have proved out in subsequent work. Perhaps the road that has been least followed is the division of the tablets into columns. We were, in a way, simply following the master, R. Campbell Thompson, whose 1930 edition of the Gilgamesh text will soon—finally—be eclipsed by the British Museum Edition scholars, especially Andrew George and I. M. Finkel.[31] That it will have taken more than seventy years to include the new material on *Gilgamesh* (and had taken nearly seventy years to edit properly what had been excavated in the 1870s) is some measure of the difficulties scholars face.

Campbell Thompson followed the tablet and column format of what is still the basis of all *Gilgamesh* editions and translations. Each of the twelve tablets is divided into six columns of text. The tendency of scholars like Andrew George has been to retain the division into tablets but not into columns, silently emending the text to approach a "standard" form. John Gardner and I had taken the other route, testing our assumption that the primary text was divided according to good aesthetic principles. We were looking for textual complexes larger than the sentence, and were pleased to see that episodes sometimes began and ended with column beginnings and endings; and sometimes episodes turned in the middle of the column. Wherever the column was sufficiently preserved, it was a functional unit. I wish the divisions of the text were recognized.

The main text, from Assurbanipal's "library," contains one stumbling-block for many scholars. The colophons are clear that the series *Gilgamesh* is complete in twelve tablets. Many find what *we* think is the epilogue to *Gilgamesh* a late, unwarranted and illogical patch on an otherwise complete work, and posit an earlier edition of the text that did not contain the notorious Twelfth Tablet. George, in his translation of the poem, ignores Tablet XII, only to translate it later in the book along with its Sumerian predecessors.

The embarrassing fact about Tablet XII is that it narrates a very different death of Enkidu and, therefore, seems completely out of place. Armed with the ancient tradition that *Gilgamesh* had been written by a certain Sîn-leqi-unninnī, a famous ancestor of a scribal school in Uruk, said to have been a *mašmašu* priest or an *ašipu*, the first word meaning an exorcist and the second, often related, a diviner, we wondered if the development of Tablet XII was a simple mistake or, rather, something of a coda.

Tablet XII opens with Gilgamesh losing two implements, the nature of which has been debated for many years. A *pukku* and a *mekkû* (XII.[i.]8–9) fall into the underworld. Enkidu brashly resolves to retrieve them. Gilgamesh advises him on what is necessary to enter the underworld safely and to withdraw. Enkidu ignores every warning and is trapped in the dreaded place. Through the intervention of the god Ea, Gilgamesh is able to summon the shade of Enkidu. The poem ends, as the Sumerian forerunners do, with a terrifying account of the underworld, in some ways like the one Enkidu gives after a dream in Tablet VII. It ends on a particularly bitter note.

What attracted us as we thought about would have seemed important to an exorcist or diviner is that Gilgamesh now has the kind of knowledge of divine secrets that was highly prized in Mesopotamia. The most obvious fact about Gilgamesh at this point is that he possesses the secret knowledge, and when he seeks more, he goes to the right place, to Ea, who knows the secrets and was the god of magic and magicians throughout Mesopotamian history. In other words, Gilgamesh approaches the level of competence of Ea himself.[32]

Secondly, although Gilgamesh is no more successful here than in earlier episodes in getting his friend back with him permanently, he—and through him, the reader—gain important insights into the world of the dead. In particular, grim though the underworld is, it allows certain people to live better than others. The person who has many sons, especially, is particularly blessed. The other world is never seen in a positive way in Mesopotamia, but the one who leaves persons behind to ease his burdens, by feeding and providing drink for the ancestor, lives there much better than one who has no one to mourn for him.

A Sumerian story, "The Death of Bilgames," has the hero making elaborate preparations for his own death, building a stone tomb and even diverting the waters of the Euphrates and then restoring its course so that the tomb built in its channel would not be found. Laid down in their places with him are his wives and children, his minstrel, attendants—even his barber (George, 206). Here Gilgamesh gets the next best thing to an answer to the question for which he was known: a detailed description of the place where he will become judge. We see, then, that the epilogue shows the hero who has found in the end the wisdom which the earlier parts of the poem had prepared us to see.

We were, at the same time, taken by a curious parallel in the early part of *Gilgamesh* with the part of the Sumerian original not translated in Tablet XII. Andrew George calls the piece "Bilgames and the Netherworld" (175–95). Whatever the *pukku* and *mekkû* are, their loss comes about when Gilgamesh so exhausts and abuses his people that they cry out for relief. This, we thought, was the original background of the motif in *Gilgamesh* where the people ask for relief and get it in the form of a rival, Enkidu. Tablet XII would, in our opinion, complete the working out of the problem. Now a wise Gilgamesh is able to resolve the problem.

I might note in passing that among the solutions proposed for a reading of *pukku* and *mekkû* is that they refer to a drum and drumstick. If they refer to a shamanic drum, that seemed quite useful and related to the context. If, as has been suggested, they are instruments of play, then the meaning was not so clear. The Sumerian story clearly makes them implements that are made from the crown and roots of a special tree, saved by Inanna, from which her bed and throne are fashioned. Gilgamesh and Enkidu rid the tree of certain spirits that have inhabited the tree, and they are then given the parts—from the top (heavens) and the roots (underworld)—to make something. With those instruments they bother the people. A suggestion by Marcelle Duchesne-Guillemin is thus far the most satisfying one offered. According to Duchesne-Guillemin, they refer to magical instruments, a scraper and its stick, used to induce trance. It is not the place here to discuss the many proposed solutions, but the trance-inducing instruments would fit the context—and they would be made of wood.

BUILDING TEXTS

The Arabs who live in the marshes near the ruins of Eridu, which the Sumerians considered the first city, still build their reed huts and larger, public structures the way they appear on ancient cylinder seals. The people and the animals they herd spend much of their lives in the shallow waters. To build on the water, the Arabs first snap the reeds at the water level, constructing a platform with reeds woven together and mud from the floor of the marsh. A rather late but very important heroic poem in Akkadian, *Enuma Elish*, tells the grim tale of fashioning a god's dwelling on that very spot. *Enuma Elish* is probably better known today for its central heroic event, the Babylonian high god Marduk's killing of the Great Mother, Tiamat. That event is foreshadowed, however, by an equally scandalous killing, in which Marduk's father, Ea, defeats the primordial father, Apsu. Both Tiamat and Apsu are imaged as the primeval waters from whose union emerge the gods who eventually overthrow the parents.

When the crafty Ea sets about fighting the old man—who has, it must be pointed out, threatened to annihilate his noisy offspring—he uses magic to still the waters.

> He poured sleep upon him [Apsu]
>   so that he was sleeping soundly,
> Put Apsu to sleep, drenched with sleep.
> Vizier Mummu the counsellor (was in) a sleepless daze.
> He [Ea] unfastened his belt, took off his crown,
> Took away his mantle of radiance and put it on himself.
> He held Apsu down and slew him.

It is at this point that Ea builds his house upon the waters. He

> Tied up Mummu and laid him across him.
> He set up his dwelling on top of Apsu,
> And grasped Mummu, held him by a nose-rope.
> When he had overcome and slain his enemies,
> Ea set up his triumphal cry over his foes.
> Then he rested very quietly inside his private quarters
> And named them Apsu and assigned chapels,
> Founded his own residence there,
> And Ea and Damkina his lover dwelt in splendour.
> In the chamber of destinies, the hall of designs,
> Bel, cleverest of the clever, sage of the gods, was begotten.
> And inside Apsu, Marduk was created;
> Inside pure Apsu, Marduk was born.[33]

Later in the same work, when Marduk has successfully defeated the Great Mother Tiamat, sliced her up, and organized the universe from her remains, he builds an even greater temple for his residence. The gods had given Marduk kingship for the benefits they would receive when he defeated the greatest of enemies, and he tested his powers by speaking a word to make a constellation disappear and speaking again to make the constellation reappear.[34]

I suspect that our modern idea of creativity, especially the creation of literary texts, is closer to Marduk's magical word that can, like God's in the Priestly Account of Creation in Genesis, bring whatever can be articulated into being. Our Greek and biblical traditions—especially in the biblical texts from the Hellenistic period—encourage us to value head-work above the work of our hands. In a time when books were made by hand, using a stylus upon wet clay or cutting signs into stone, however, I am increasingly persuaded that Mesopotamian writers had the other model in mind. The writers certainly appreciated a well-crafted text, especially since the difficult cuneiform system of writing required many years to master.

In another myth that involved the god Ea, whose Sumerian name was Enki, over one hundred of the divine words, or *me*, are listed in four different parts of the text. (I liken the *me* to the operating system of a computer.) One sequence in the poem is particularly striking, since it locates the writer firmly in a group of craftsmen (perhaps originally craftswomen):

> the craft of the carpenter,
> the craft of the copper-worker,
> the craft of the scribe,
> the craft of the smith,
> the craft of the leather-worker,
> the craft of the fuller,
> the craft of the builder,
> the craft of the reed-worker.[35]

The earliest texts that have been discovered, from Uruk in the late fourth millennium, at the very invention of true writing, tell us that these and other workers who contributed to the extraordinary development of the Mesopotamian city state, were as valued as the priests and rulers. Headwork and handwork were not differentiated as they came to be in the West. (Or to use a different principle used by sociologists, such as in the famous Middletown project, the Sumerians did not divide labor between those who work with people and those who work with objects.[36]) With Gilgamesh we are faced with a hero who is remembered not only for the leadership and courage required to perform great, memorable feats of strength and cunning, but also one who combines headwork and handwork in the two activities that mark him above his peers: writing texts and building walls.

WRITING AND THE PSEUDOLITHIC IMAGINATION

Early Mesopotamian tradition, especially, reminds us that wisdom is not necessarily connected with writing. Utnapishtim *tells* Gilgamesh a story and in it recounts how Ea *told* him what to do and even how to con his fellow citizens into building the ark. The Sumerians knew the power of the divine *me*, most powerful words. In a Sumerian myth, "Inanna and Enki," the god of wisdom himself is tricked or seduced by Inanna/ Ishtar into giving up the *me* in his possession. She takes them with her successfully back to Uruk.[37] In Sumerian thought, intellect and understanding are embodied, not separated from the body, as they will become in the Western tradition; and the key term is *geštú*, the ear, since reason and comprehension, given to humans by the gods, passes through the ear.[38] This is a view that might be expected in a society in which very few persons in any era would be able to read and write.

The complexity of the cuneiform writing system, in contrast with the later alphabet that developed from it, kept it literally in the hands of a few specialists. It took many years of schooling to master cuneiform. A few kings boast of their literacy—but the small number undoubtedly means that such ability was rare among monarchs. But scribes—I prefer to call them writers—were essential to the running of a complex state, and from Archaic Uruk times, writers were close to the powers in both temple and palace. Indeed, a Sumerian poem deals with the invention of writing (in Uruk), as the last of a series of tests passed by the leader of Uruk.[39] His rival, who challenges him, is given a tablet to read and sees only the scratchings of nails—that is, the wedge-shaped characters that gave cuneiform its name—and gives up trying to best the Sumerian.

The Sumerians would have appreciated the name for true writing given it by Marvin Powell: *homo literatus sumericus Urukeus*, after its invention in the last centuries of the fourth millennium B.C.E.[40] The closest Sumerian and Akkadian came to a concept of knowledge or science was *tupšarrutu*, the art of the *dubsar*, or scribe, something like tabletology (Vanstiphout, 2191).[41] In our *Gilgamesh*, written of course long after the invention of writing, the tablet even appears in the underworld. In Enkidu's dream in Tablet VII Enkidu sees a group of priests, Ereshkigal herself, and before her Belet-seri, the scribe of the underworld, holding a tablet and reading aloud.

It is, however, Gilgamesh the writer that is important for our purposes. Unlike the tablets containing the versions of Gilgamesh—and thousands of other texts—made of clay, sometimes oven-baked but mainly baked in the sun, the tablets Gilgamesh is said to have inscribed are of stone (I.i.8). A tablet-box (I.i.25) is said to contain his story, and it is a very precious stone tablet, of lapis lazuli. The two references to stone tablets frame the view of Uruk that appears in the prologue and again at the end of Tablet XI: the walls of Uruk. The monumental architecture—temples, ziggurats, and palaces—of Sumer is mostly made of brick, a necessity in the resource-poor flood plain on which the cities were built. *Gilgamesh* claims that the great city walls were not only ancient, its foundation established by the Seven Sages, but are built up not of fill but of oven-fired bricks. It is an image of permanence in a world increasingly disturbed by change—not the least of which was the historic need of city walls for defense in an age that saw the organization of warfare on a scale that had not been seen before. The heroic king so much admired in history emerged in just such a setting. Archaeologists have long designated early eras as Old Stone and New Stone ages. The writing culture of Uruk appears in what I would call a pseudolithic age. Stone may represent the ideal, but clay—tablets, pots, tools, and especially bricks—allowed the cities of the south to flourish. The recognition of humble clay comes in the very definition of Uruk, with its parts equally divided into dwellings, date-groves, and clay-pits. As I read the poem, it is important that the magnificent city walls are balanced within by the sacred precinct of Ishtar, whose temple is said to spread through a half of a square mile.

The Epic Voice in Gilgamesh

At the beginning of this reading of *Gilgamesh*, I mentioned that John Gardner and I were skeptical of the tendency among scholars to consider the work an epic. Particularly if one focuses too intently on certain formal features of the Western epics—conventions like calling upon the muse, developing epic similes, stating the theme, and beginning *in medias res*—the label "epic" is as likely to obscure as it is to illuminate the inner workings of the piece. In fact, the last two epic conventions *are* to be found in *Gilgamesh*, and a parallel to Homer's "rosy-fingered Dawn" also appears. Conversely, the Western epic tradition includes as much diversity as conformity to rules of genre. One need only think of *Orlando Furioso*, *Jerusalem Delivered*, Edmund Spenser's attempt to "fashion a gentleman" in allegorical romance modes, and John Milton's justifying the ways of God to men to see the flexibility the "epic" genre has allowed.

It is increasingly clear that the Standard Version of *Gilgamesh* announces itself as about wisdom. Andrew George translates the opening lines, which have been restored only recently, as follows:

> He who saw the Deep, the country's foundation,
> [who] knew..., was wise in all matters!
> [Gilgamesh, who] saw the Deep, the country's foundation
> [who] knew..., was wise in all matters! (George, 1)

For some reason the poet, in using the term *nagbu*, which George translates as "the Deep," avoids one of the few Sumerian words that has managed to move steadily through Akkadian, Greek, and then into modern Indo-European languages, including English, as "abyss." I still think that Gilgamesh saw what we think is the abyss, though the word is not *apsû*, the Akkadian borrowing of *abzu*. The *nagbu* is a spring or fountain, or the underground waters that are the source of springs and rivers. The *Chicago Assyrian Dictionary* has many citations that show the god Ea, *šar apsî*, or king of the *abzu*, as the master of the waters of the Deep, *mê nagbi* (11/2.110). But the *nagbu* was also poetically "totality," the "all" (11/2.111). In good epic fashion, then, the poet opens *Gilgamesh* with the powerful theme: Gilgamesh is the one who has seen everything. Moreover, this is immediately followed by what John Gardner and I thought then and I still consider the key lines, the emphasis on the hero's *learning* wisdom, mainly through suffering. What differentiated Gilgamesh from other early heroes was that he *wrote* his experiences. This is the Gilgamesh I have emphasized here: the one

> who saw things secret, opened the place hidden,
> and carried back word of the time before the Flood—
> he travelled the road, exhausted, in pain,
> and cut his works into a stone tablet. (I.i.)

The recently restored first lines once again return to the question of the "land" Gilgamesh came to know. George likes "the country's foundation" (*matu*)—but what is this "country?" What are the *epic* implications of Gilgamesh's hard wisdom, particularly his learning what it is to lead the city of Uruk? Adele Berlin, who took an ethnopoetic approach to the early Sumerian epics, pointed out that the focus on Uruk was not incompatible with a Sumerian view of the entire nation. The earliest Sumerian epics were already less concerned with poeticized history than with "their values, their role models, their conceptions of the past, and, by extension, their conception of their national identity."[42] Even before Utuhegal of Uruk overthrew the Gutians, the enemies of the Sumerians; and reestablished Sumerian hegemony in southern Mesopotamia, Uruk and its heroes were at the center of national identity.

The most conspicuous case of fronting, or foregrounding, material in *Gilgamesh* has been known at least since Jeffrey Tigay made a careful survey of the different Gilgamesh traditions in *The Evolution of the Gilgamesh Epic*.[43] The first twenty-six lines of the poem, much of which introduces the frame—the walls of Uruk and the sacred precinct within the walls—and is completed at the end of Tablet XI, stand in sharp contrast to the older opening of the poem.

We know that an Old Babylonian version began with a paean to Gilgamesh the famous, powerfully built military hero, the very pattern of strength, the opener of the mountain passes. "Who like Gilgamesh can boast, 'I am the king!'?" (I.i.44).

Boasting of one's strength and gaining a "name" through courageous deeds like challenging Humbaba and the Bull of Heaven are central to the Western epic tradition. They have their place in this version of the Gilgamesh tradition. Those words, captured in cuneiform signs, have been overwritten here by the writer who cut his pain into a tablet and gave distinctive voice to the heroic tradition.

JOHN MAIER
State University of New York/Brockport

NOTES

1. John Maier, "What Happened to Sam-kha in *The Epic of Gilgameš? Literary Onomastics Studies* 2 (1975).
2. Simo Parpola, *Assyrian Prophecies* (Helsinki: University Press, 1997), L. The text is given on pp. 40–41.
3. In his review of Parpola's *Assyrian Prophecies,* Jerrold Cooper reads these lines, not as Parpola had, as the utterance of the suffering ecstatic, but as the voice of Ishtar herself. See "Assyrian Prophecies, the Assyrian Tree, and the Mesopotamian Origins of Jewish Monotheism, Greek Philosophy, Christian Theology, Gnosticism, and Much More," *Journal of the American Oriental Society* 120 (2000): 44. In either case, extraordinary effort (especially for a goddess) is expended to preserve the life of the (human) king.
4. Unless otherwise noted, quotations are from John Gardner and John Maier, *Gilgamesh, Translated from the Sîn-leqi-unninnī Version* (New York: Alfred A. Knopf, 1984). Compare Andrew George, *The Epic of Gilgamesh, A New Translation* (New York: Barnes and Noble Books, 1999), p. 95. Parenthetical references in the text are to this edition. Neither George nor Simo Parpola, *The Standard Babylonian Epic of Gilgamesh* (Helsinki: The Neo-Assyrian Text Corpus Project, 1997), 111, divide Tablet XI into columns; the line numbers are slightly different (George = ll. 198–203; Parpola = 197–202).
5. For the wife's speech, George = ll. 214–17; Parpola, *Standard,* = ll. 213–16.
6. George = ll. 271–73; Parpola, *Standard,* 267–69.
7. Ludmila Zeman, *The Last Quest of Gilgamesh* (Montreal: Tundra Books, 1995), n.p.
8. See Richard A. Henshaw, *Female and Male: The Cultic Personnel* (Allison Park, Pennsylvania: Pickwick Publications, 1994), p. 217, and Appendix 4, "What Happened in the ès-dam/ astammu-House?"

9. In two thorough analyses, Tzvi Abusch details the differences between the Old Babylonian and Standard Babylonian versions of Siduri's advice to Gilgamesh. See Abusch, "Gilgamesh's Request and Siduri's Denial" (Part I), *The Tablet and the Scroll: Near Eastern Studies in Honor of W. W. Hallo*, ed. M. E. Cohen, et al. (Bethesda, MD: CDL, 1993), 1–14, and "Gilgamesh's Request and Siduri's Denial, Part II: An Analysis and Interpretation of an Old Babylonian Fragment about Mourning and Celebration," *Journal of the Ancient Near Eastern Society of Columbia University* 22 (1993): 3–17.

10. George considers the Stone Ones the companions of Urshanabi and reads, not urnu-snakes but "*picks a pine clean.*" See George, *Gilgamesh*, p. 79.

11. See Igor M. Diakonoff and N. B. Jankowska, "An Elamite Gilgames Text from Argistihenele, Urartu (Armavirblur, 8th century B.C.)" *Zeitschrift für Assyriologie* 80 (1990): 102-24; also Robert Temple, "Introduction to *He Who Saw Everything*" (London: Rider, 1991), vii-ix; rpt. John Maier, ed. *Gilgamesh: A Reader* (Wauconda, Illinois: Bolchazy-Carducci, 1997), pp. 321–22.

12. For a discussion of the earliest Gilgamesh texts, from EDIII, see Douglas R. Frayne, "The Birth of Gilgames in Ancient Mesopotamian Art," *Bulletin of the Canadian Society for Mesopotamian Studies* 34 (1999), 39–49. "The Early Dynastic Hymn to Gilgames" does not clearly specify how the "herb-pot of life" is obtained, or lost, though a line does indicate a field-meadow where the herb-pot is set on the banks of a river.

13. Tikva Frymer-Kensky, *In the Wake of the Goddesses: Women, Culture and the Biblical Transformation of Pagan Myth* (New York: Free Press, 1992); her chapter on "The Marginalization of the Goddesses" is reprinted in Maier, *Gilgamesh: A Reader*, 95–108. Rivka Harris, "Images of Women in the Gilgamesh Epic," has been reprinted in *Gilgamesh: A Reader*, 79–94, and again in her *Gender and Aging in Mesopotamia* (Norman: University of Oklahoma Press, 2000), pp. 119–28.

14. Parpola has noted that Ishtar appears as convener of the divine assembly, and that her behavior in bringing about the flood is like Tiamat's inclination to destroy her noisy offspring in *Enuma Elish*. See Parpola, *Assyrian Prophecies*, LXXXV.

15. For the gods as learning from the flood, see Bernard F. Batto, *Slaying the Dragon: Mythmaking in the Biblical Tradition* (Louisville: Westminster/ John Knox, 1992), pp. 41–71; reprinted in Maier, *Gilgamesh: A Reader*, 245–59.

16. In these two instances, Ishtar acts like the biblical deity in first, remembering the flood—the turning point in the story—and then vowing never to forget it (Genesis 8:20-9:17). See *Gilgamesh*, 243–44 and John Maier, "The Flood Story: Four Literary Approaches," *Approaches to Teaching the Hebrew Bible as Literature in Translation*, ed. Barry N. Olshen and Yael S. Feldman (New York: Modern Language Association, 1989), pp. 110–13.

17. Henshaw, *Female and Male*, Appendix 4 (191–270), with lengthy discussions of "sacred prostitution" and the so-called "sacred marriage."

18. The proverb collection, "Instructions of Suruppak," ends with a sharp contrast between those nomads and mountain men who do not eat grain or build houses like people from the city. The extremes are mediated by the farmers and shepherds, who would seem to provide a bridge to "civilized" life. See Bendt Alster, *The Instructions of Suruppak: A Sumerian Proverb Collection* (Copenhagen: Akademisk Forlag, 1974), pp. 48–51.
19. Both versions of the story involve Enki in an important way, as do the variants of "Bilgames and the Netherworld." See George, Gilgamesh, pp. 149–66; 175–208.
20. Samuel Noah Kramer and John Maier, *Myths of Enki, The Crafty God* (New York: Oxford University Press, 1989), pp. 199–202.
21. For the proverb collections, see Bendt Alster, *Proverbs of Ancient Sumer: The World's Earliest Proverb Collections*, 2 vols. (Bethesda, Maryland: CDL Press, 1997). For the place of proverbs in the Mesopotamian schools, see Niek Veldhuis, "Sumerian Proverbs in their Curricular Context," *Journal of the American Oriental Society* 120 (2000): 383–99. A variety of "wisdom" texts are found in W. G. Lambert, *Babylonian Wisdom Literature* (Oxford: Clarendon, 1960).
22. Andrew George, "What's New in the Gilgamesh Epic?" *The Canadian Society for Mesopotamian Studies Bulletin* 34 (1999): 56.
23. The place of the offering (on the roof) may suggest a very ancient Mesopotamian temple, since the stairs to the roof over the sanctuary disappeared early in the third millennium B.C.E. Cf. Yasuyoshi Okada, "An Architectural Innovation of the Temple Style: Sumerian to Babylonian," *Priests and Officials in the Ancient Near East*, ed. Kazuko Watanabe (Heidelberg: Universitätsverlag C. Winter, 1999), p. 50.
24. Walter Burkert, *The Orientalizing Revolution: Near Eastern Influence on Greek Culture in the Early Archaic Age*, trans. Margaret E. Pinder and Walter Burkert (Cambridge, MA: Harvard University Press, 1992); rpt. John Maier, ed. *Gilgamesh: A Reader* (Wauconda, IL: Bolchazy-Carducci, 1997), 182.
25. Parpola, *Assyrian Prophecies*, xviii–xlv.
26. Parpola's interpretation of the evidence for Assyrian monotheism has been challenged by Jerrold Cooper (see above), but it is possible that the prominence of a male figure and a female counterpart (chief "aspect" or "attribute"?) was the pattern much earlier, such as in Old Akkadian, where Il ("God") and Ashtar (a form of Ishtar) are mentioned, but the many gods and goddesses that appear later are not evident. See Walther Sallaberg and Aage Westenholz, *Mesopotamien: Akkade-Zeit und Ur III-Zeit* (Freiburg: Universitätsverlag, 1999), p. 78.
27. For a thorough discussion, see Tzvi Abusch, "Ishtar's Proposal and Gilgamesh's Refusal: An Interpretation of The Gilgamesh Epic, Tablet 6, Lines 1–79," *History of Religions* 26 (1986): 143–97.
28. Burkert, in Maier, *Gilgamesh: A Reader*, pp. 179–80.
29. For the *en* and *lugal*, see William W. Hallo, *Early Mesopotamian Royal Titles: A Philologic and Historical Analysis* (New Haven: American Oriental Society, 1957), pp. 3–13; and for the Archaic Uruk period in

particular, see D. Schmandt-Besserat, "Images of Enship," *Between the Rivers and over the Mountains*, ed. M. Frantipane, et al. (Rome: University of Rome Press, 1993), pp. 201–20.

30. Piotr Steinkeller traces the complex evolution of the *en*, its traditional association with Uruk, and the relationships among titles *en*, *lugal*, and *ensik* in "On Rulers, Priests and Sacred Marriage: Tracing the Evolution of Early Sumerian Kingship," *Priests and Officials in the Ancient Near East*, ed. Kazuko Watanabe (Heidelberg: Universitätsverlag C. Winter, 1999), pp. 203–38, esp. p.112.

31. R. Campbell Thompson, *The Epic of Gilgamesh: Text, Transliteration, and Notes* (Oxford: Clarendon Press, 1930).

32. Associations between Gilgamesh and the god of Eridu, Enki/Ea, are strengthened as new versions of Gilgamesh stories are edited. Steinkeller speculates that the earliest Sumerian pantheon was dominated by female deities and one male figure, Enki, who "undoubtedly was the original head of the pantheon" (113). For the god and the traditions associated with Eridu, see Kramer and Maier, *Myths of Enki, The Crafty God*, and William W. Hallo, "Enki and the Theology of Eridu," *Journal of the American Oriental Society* 116 (1996): 231–35.

33. Stephanie Dalley, *Myths from Mesopotamia* (Oxford: University Press, 1989), p. 235.

34. Dalley, *Myths from Mesopotamia*, p. 250.

35. Samuel Noah Kramer and John Maier, *Myths of Enki, The Crafty God* (New York: Oxford University Press, 1989), pp. 62–63.

36. Robert S. Lynd and Helen Merrell Lynd, *Middletown: A Study in American Culture* (New York: Harcourt, Brace and Co., 1956), p. 22. There they distinguish basically Working Class and Business Class groups, those who "address their activities in getting a living primarily to *things*, utilizing material tools in the making of things and the performance of service, while the members of the second group address their activities predominantly to *people* in the selling or promotion of things, services, and ideas."

37. See Kramer and Maier, *Myths of Enki*, pp. 57–69.

38. Julia M. Asher-Greve and A. Lawrence Asher, "From Thales to Foucault...and back to Sumer," *43rd Recontre assyriologique internationale, Prague, 1996* (Prague: Oriental Institute, 1998), p. 39.

39. Enmerkar, in two Sumerian poems, the better known of which is *Enmerkar and the Lord of Aratta* is credited with the invention of writing. Ironically, Gilgamesh and his father Lugalbanda, of the three "heroes" of Uruk, were praised in the tradition for writing out their experiences, while Enmerkar, far from being praised, was discredited, along with the Akkadian king, Naram-Sin, and the reason appears to be that he did not leave a stele for later persons to read. See the treatment of Enmerkar in "Naram-Sin and the Enemy Hordes," in Joan Goodnick Westenholz, *Legends of the Kings of Akkade* (Winona Lake, Indiana: Eisenbrauns, 1997), pp. 284–89.

40. Herman Vanstiphout, "Memory and Literacy in Ancient Western Asia," *Civilizations of the Ancient Near East*, ed. Jack M. Sasson, et al. (New York: Charles Scribner's Sons, 1995), p. 2182.

41. Vanstiphout, "Memory and Literacy in Ancient Western Asia," *Civilizations of the Ancient Near East*, p. 2191.

42. Adele Berlin, "Ethnopoetry and the Enmerkar Epics," *Journal of the American Oriental Society* 103 (1983): 17–24. See also Joan Goodnick Westenholz, "Cult of Dead Heroes," discussed in *Gilgamesh*, 60, and her essay, "Heroes of Akkad," *Journal of the American Oriental Society* 103 (1983): 327–36.

43. Jeffrey H. Tigay, *The Evolution of the Gilgamesh Epic* (Philadelphia: University of Pennsylvania Press, 1982), pp. 140–60, 261–65 (rpt. in *Gilgamesh: A Reader*, 40–49). See *Gilgamesh*, 59–60.

RECENT TRANSLATIONS OF GILGAMESH

Dalley, Stephanie. *Myths from Mesopotamia.* Oxford: Oxford University Press, 1989.

Foster, Benjamin, ed. *The Epic of Gilgamesh*, A Norton Critical Edition. New York: W. W. Norton, 2001.

Gardner, John, and Maier, John. *Gilgamesh*, Translated from the Sîn-leqi-unninni Version. New York: Knopf, 1984.

George, Andrew. *The Epic of Gilgamesh: A New Translation.* London: Penguin, 1999.

Kovacs, Maureen Gallery. *The Epic of Gilgamesh.* Stanford: Stanford University Press, 1985.

SUGGESTIONS FOR FURTHER READING

Abusch, Tzvi. "Gilgamesh's Request and Siduri's Denial" (Part I). *The Tablet and the Scroll: Near Eastern Studies in Honor of W. W. Hallo.* Ed. M. E. Cohen, et al. Bethesda, Maryland: CDL, 1993. 1–14; "Gilgamesh's Request and Siduri's Denial. Part II: An Analysis and Interpretation of an Old Babylonian Fragment about Mourning and Celebration." *Journal of the Ancient Near Eastern Society of Columbia University* 22 (1993): 3–17.

Batto, Bernard F. *Slaying the Dragon: Mythmaking in the Biblical Tradition.* Louisville: Westminster/ John Knox, 1992.

Beye, Charles R. "The Epic of Gilgamesh, the Bible, and Homer. Some Narrative Parallels." *Mnemai. Classical Studies in Memory of Karl K. Hulley.* Ed. Harold D. Evjen. Chico: Scholars Press, 1984. 7–20.

Bottéro, Jean. *Mesopotamia: Writing, Reasoning and the Gods.* Trans. Zainab Bahrani and Marc Van de Mieroop. Chicago: University of Chicago Press, 1992.

Burkert, Walter. *The Orientalizing Revolution: Near Eastern Influence on Greek Culture in the Early Archaic Age.* Trans. Margaret E. Pinder and Walter Burkert. Cambridge: Harvard University Press, 1992.

Dalley, Stephanie, ed. *The Legacy of Mesopotamia.* Oxford: Oxford University Press, 1998.

Damrosch, David. *The Narrative Covenant: Transformations of Genre in the Growth of Biblical Literature.* Ithaca: Cornell University Press, 1987.

Gresseth, Gerald K. "The Gilgamesh Epic and Homer." *Classical Journal* 70 (1974-75): 1–18.

Hallo, William W. *Origins: The Ancient Near Eastern Background of Some Modern Western Institutions.* Leiden: E. J. Brill, 1996.

Jacobsen, Thorkild. "The Gilgamesh Epic: Tragic and Romantic Vision." *Lingering Over Words: Studies in Ancient Near Eastern Literature in Honor of William L. Moran.* Ed. Tzvi Abusch, et al. Atlanta: Scholars Press, 1990. 231–50.

Jager, Bernd. "The Gilgamesh Epic: A Phenomenological Exploration." *Review of Existential Psychology and Psychiatry* 12 (1973): 1–43.

Kuhrt, Amélie, and Sherwin-White, Susan, ed. *Hellenism in the East: The Interaction of Greek and Non-Greek Civilizations from Syria to Central Asia after Alexander.* Berkeley: University of California Press, 1987.

Kluger, Rivkah Schärf. *The Archetypal Significance of Gilgamesh, A Modern Hero.* Ed. H. Yehezkel Kluger. Einsiedeln: Daimon Verlag, 1991.

Kramer, Samuel Noah, and Maier, John. *Myths of Enki, The Crafty God.* New York: Oxford University Press, 1989.

Lambert, "Gilgames in Religious, Historical and Omen Texts and the Historicity of Gilgames." Gilgames et sa légende. Paris: Imprimerie Nationale and Librarie C. Klincksieck, 1960. 39–56.

Maier, John, ed. *Gilgamesh: A Reader.* Wauconda, Illinois: Bolchazy-Carducci, 1997.

Oppenheim, A. Leo. "Mesopotamian Mythology, 1–3." *Orientalia* 16 (1947): 207–38; 17 (1948): 15–58; 19 (1950): 129–58.

Parpola, Simo. "The Assyrian Tree of Life: Tracing the Origins of Jewish Monotheism and Greek Philosophy." *Journal of Near Eastern Studies* 52 (1993): 161–208.

Pruyser, Paul W., and Luke, J. Tracy. "The Epic of Gilgamesh." *American Imago* 39 (1982): 73–93.

Richardson, Miles. "Gilgamesh and Christ: Two Contradictory Images of Man in Search of a Better World." *Aspects of Cultural Change.* Ed. Joseph Aceves. pp. 7–20. Athens, Georgia: University of Georgia Press, 1972.

Ricoeur, Paul. *The Symbolism of Evil.* Trans. Emerson Buchanan. Boston: Beacon Press, 1969.

Sasson, Jack M., ed. *Civilizations of the Ancient Near East.* 4 Vols. New York: Charles Scribner's Sons, 1995.

Tigay, Jeffrey H. *The Evolution of the Gilgamesh Epic.* Philadelphia: University of Pennsylvania Press, 1982.

Vanstiphout, Herman L. J. "The Craftsmanship of Sîn-leqi-unninnī." *Orientalia Lovaniensia Periodica* 21 (1990): 45–79.

Veenker, Ronald A. "Gilgamesh and the Magic Plant." *Biblical Archaeologist* 44 (1981): 199–205.

Vulpe, Nicola. "Irony and the Unity of the Gilgamesh Epic." *Journal of Near Eastern Studies* 53 (1994): 275–83.

Westenholz, Joan Goodnick. "Towards a New Conceptualization of the Female Role in Mesopotamian Society." *Journal of the American Oriental Society* 110 (1990): 510–21.

West, M. L. *The East Face of Helicon: West Asiatic Elements in Greek Poetry and Myth.* Oxford: Clarendon, 1997.

Wolff, Hope Nash. *A Study in the Narrative Structure of Three Epic Poems: "Gilgamesh," the "Odyssey," "Beowulf."* New York: Garland, 1987.

DISCUSSION QUESTIONS

Gilgamesh is revered for the building of walls and the inscribing of wisdom. Are the two related?

The city of Uruk is described as being composed of three parts. Gilgamesh too is divided into thirds: two-thirds human one one-third mortal. Is there a possible connection here between Gilgamesh and the city? Is the city too part human and part divine?

The tyranny of Gilgamesh. What is its source? What happens to it? When he returns to Uruk, does he return to Uruk as king, as tyrant?

Why does Enkidu, fresh from the forest, immediately stand against Gilgamesh? Why is he so opposed to the privileges Gilgamesh is accustomed to enjoying?

What do we make of Gilgamesh's rejection of Ishtar? Is it reasonable, arrogant, or cowardly? Even if he is right in linking her bed with his grave, i.e., even though he realizes that becoming her consort will mean his accepting his own death, is he not refusing his royal duty as king and his fate as human in denying her. Isn't it his responsibility to lie with her as king and to go down into death as a human being?

For seven days and seven nights Enkidu made love with the love-priestess Shamhat, while Gilgamesh rejected the love-goddess Ishtar. What is the significance of their conflicting responses to these offers of love?

After the death of his friend and companion Enkidu, Gilgamesh wanders the wilderness, becoming in some ways a wild man himself. He seems to mimic the condition of Enkidu before Enkidu encountered the prostitute and entered the city? What is the significance of Gilgamesh's retracing the path of Enkidu, and in reverse?

Gilgamesh is tested by Utnapishtim to see whether he can resist sleep. How does this relate to Gilgamesh's desire to resist death?

What are we to conclude from the story of Gilgamesh? That we are to embrace human limits, or that we should strive against them?

If wisdom comes from suffering and mortality, how can we account for the wisdom of the gods? Are the gods wise? Are they models for human imitation?

Discussion Points

• The initial ambiguity of Gilgamesh's and Enkidu's humanity.

• The stages of Enkidu's humanization by Shamhat.

• The preliminary aloneness/alienation of Gilgamesh and Enkidu contrasted with the friendship they later discover in each other.

• The different attitudes of Gilgamesh, on the one hand, and Enkidu, on the other, to the 'great deed' of entering the cedar forest to slay Humbaba.

• The dying words of Enkidu in the light of what follows, i.e., the quest of Gilgamesh and its outcome.

• The range of female characters in the poem and their relationship with Gilgamesh and Enkidu.

• The encounter with Siduri and its place in the story.

• The numerous 'solutions' to mortality present in *Gilgamesh*.

Points for Further Investigation

• Gilgamesh is two-thirds divine and one-third human. His mother is divine and his father is human.

• In the early versions of the story, Enkidu was a minor character of little note. He was to Gilgamesh merely a servant, a squire.

• Enkidu, as portrayed in the poem, is a Mesopotamian image of primal human being, an Adam of sorts.

• Enkidu, when his death is near, has second thoughts about having become human. He gives his reasons for this, and he is seemingly refuted or at least silenced.

• The story of Utnapishtim and the Great Flood was not a part of the early epic.

• The flood story is common to both Gilgamesh and the Hebrew Bible, and the accounts are quite similar. Shamash is the Sumerian sun-god; and the Hebrew word for sun is *shemesh*.

• The story of Gilgamesh seems to be about becoming human. Being human is held up as something to be accepted, even striven after, perhaps even celebrated. But there is little joy in the poem.

• The closing lines of the Gilgamesh repeat its opening lines. The poem is a circle.

DAVID

For the second of our two ancient texts, we turn to the Israelite story of King David, as it is presented to us in the books of 1 and 2 Samuel and the first two chapters of 1 Kings from the Hebrew Bible. According to Jewish tradition, this material formed the third part and the very beginning of the fourth part of the section of the Bible known as the Former Prophets and was attributed to the prophets Samuel, for whom this section of the Bible was named, and Nathan, who figures importantly in the story of David itself. But as Robert Alter demonstrates so effectively—in his masterful translation of and commentary on the David story, and in the following essay—whoever wrote it, the story of David clearly stands on its own as a masterpiece of world literature. Here we are presented with the unforgettable story of the young shepherd boy who, through a mixture of bravado, political cunning, and personal charisma, rises to the position of King of all Israel and becomes the founder of Israel's Davidic dynasty. As Alter notes, in presenting a crucial early chapter in the on-going formation of Israel as a distinct people and nation-state, the story of David's meteoric rise to power and his stormy and sometimes ruthless reign as king surely constitutes one of the great historical novels and political sagas of all time.

BIBLICAL TIMELINE

1800–1700	Abraham and Sarah
1700–1600	Isaac, Jacob, Joseph
1600–1300	Moses and the Exodus
1200–1100	Judges, Joshua, Deborah
1100–1000	Kingship: Samuel, Saul
1000–961	King David: United Kingdom
961–922	Reign of King Solomon
922–722	Northern Monarchy of Israel Prophet Elijah (ca. 850)
922–587	Southern Monarchy of Judah Prophet Isaiah (ca. 742–700)
622	Rediscovery of Deuteronomic History
700–600	Assyrian Occupation of Northern Kingdom Prophet Jeremiah (ca. 626–587)
600–525	Babylonian Conquest and Exile Prophet Ezekiel (ca. 593–573)
587	Fall of Jerusalem & Destruction of Temple
525–336	Persian Conquest of Babylon, Return from Exile, Temple Rebuilt
336–323	Greek Conquest, Alexander the Great
323–100	Hellenism
168–63	Maccabean Period

B.C.E.
_____
C.E.

70	Destruction of the Second Temple and Roman Occupation

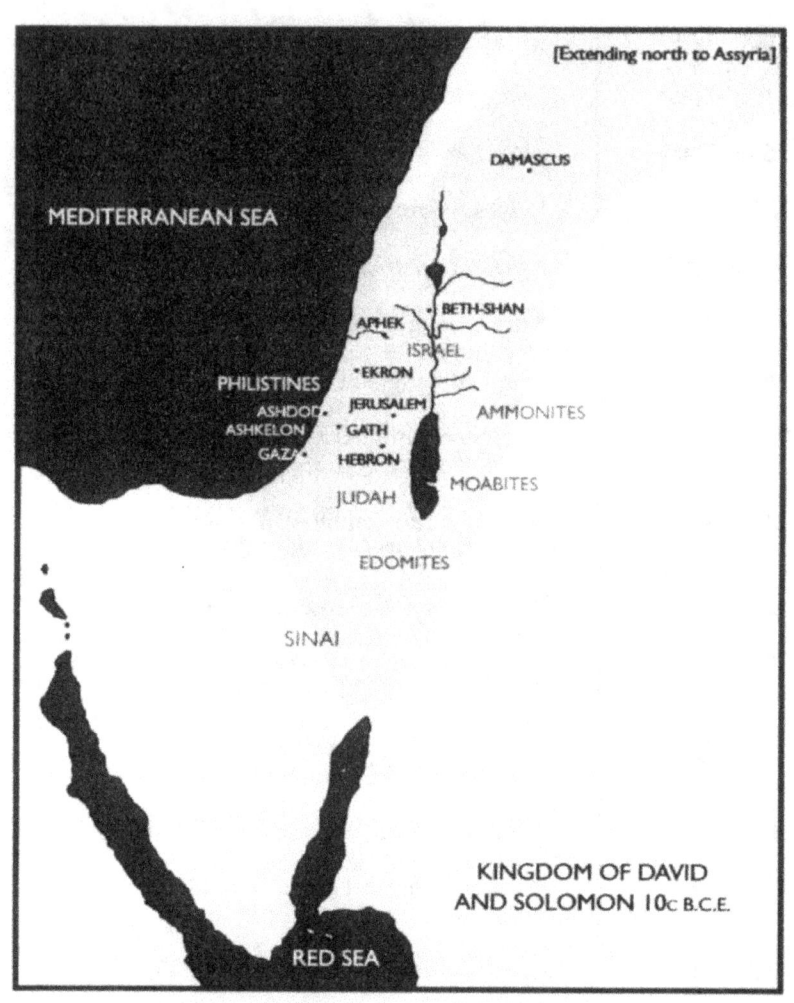

DAVIDIC KINGDOM

THE DAVID STORY

"The story of David is probably the greatest single narrative representation in antiquity of a human life evolving by slow stages through time, shaped and altered by the pressures of political life, public institutions, family, the impulses of body and spirit, the eventual sad decay of the flesh. It also provides the most unflinching insight into the cruel processes of history and into human behavior warped by the pursuit of power. And nowhere is the Bible's astringent narrative economy, its ability to define characters and etch revelatory dialogue in a few telling strokes, more brilliantly deployed."[1]

As you heard from this little quotation just now from the introduction that I wrote to *The David Story*, I am deeply convinced as a reader, that is someone who reads not only ancient literature but a lot of modern literature, that this is altogether one of the greatest stories we have. It is virtually unique in ancient literature as far as I can see, with the partial exception of the story of Jacob and Joseph, in doing precisely what you heard indicated in the sentence quoted—in showing how a human life changes through time. And I would just remind you of the span that we see in the story of David. At the beginning, he is a charming young man from the provinces, very charismatic, loved by everyone, who becomes an endearing young military hero. Then he is thrust out from the court by King Saul, and he has to live as a fugitive in the badlands. And very quickly, as you can see in some of those episodes, he becomes a kind of battle-hardened guerilla chieftain. Then we see him consolidating power, uniting the country under a single monarchy, and in a way which we will look at more closely further on, he becomes a sedentary monarch and, to some extent, the victim of the sedentary monarchy. And then this very powerful figure turns into an aging man who seems to be at the mercy of his own fierce sons, finally in fact thrust into flight and exile by one rebel son, Absalom. At the very end of the trajectory, in that poignant moment just before the end of David's life, we see him shivering in bed, a frail old man, maybe not with his wits all together either, since I have a strong suspicion that Nathan the Prophet and Bathsheba bamboozled him about who is to be the successor to the throne.

If you compare that, let us say, to Odysseus—and here I am hearkening back as some of you will recognize, to what Eric Auerbach says about Odysseus in the first chapter of his great work

Mimesis—Odysseus goes through twenty years of experience, ten years in the siege of Troy and ten years on the sea, until finally he gets back to Ithaca—and he hardly seems to have changed.[2] There is certainly something perhaps heartening in such human resilience, but in the end it is a representation of human life less attuned to what time does to us, and what our experience in time and our own bodies do to us, than what we find in the case of David. So this for me is one measure of the greatness of the David story.

The second measure is that this is one of the profound narratives we have in the Western tradition about what it is to be a political animal: about how human beings behave in the arena of politics, how the pressures of political institutions affect character and moral behavior, what is involved in the ruthless drive to power, what are the kinds of moral compromises one has to make in order to obtain and then preserve power. All these troubling and multi-faceted aspects of life in the political realm are represented with extraordinary subtlety in this story. I would say that for me as a reader there may be four or five great texts like this in the Western tradition. I would line it up with Stendahl's *The Charter House of Parma*, perhaps Dostoyevsky's *The Possessed*, and only one or two others. And I find that as much as our political institutions have changed, and certain decorums of social intercourse have changed, that there is a lot about this story that still speaks to our political situation in the twenty-first century.

So what I would like to do, then, is to give you a little bit of an overview of the David story, and then with a kind of zoom lens, move in to what I think is the pivotal episode in the whole story. And it is pivotal. I am not using this term loosely. I think it applies in a precise structural sense—for the David story pointedly breaks in two. By the way, I should say parenthetically that there are scholars who will break it into a lot more than two parts, because they see it as a composite of many different sources. To be sure, as with most biblical texts, certain disparate materials have been incorporated into the narrative, but these are quite circumscribed in scope. I myself remain resolutely unconvinced that, as some scholars claim, there is an entirely discrete story of the young David, a wholly distinct Succession Narrative, and three or four other sub-narratives. In fact I think that the story of Saul is inseparable from the story of David, and that you lose a great deal if you do not see the one continuous whole.

So, let us go back to the notion of a pivot. I think the story breaks into two large units, as a kind of diptych, with the pivotal moment being the story of David and Bathsheba. Before that moment, we see David progressively consolidating power. And the way that is represented is, I think, extremely instructive in terms of this being a political narrative—I am inclined to say, the first political novel. It might take us too far afield for me to try to explain what all this has to do with history writing, but let us propose a brief generalization: I do not think this kind of narrative should be thought of as a fabrication or fiction, plain and simple; it is rather an attempt to grasp the inner meaning of a set of historical events by reconstructing them imaginatively, as for example, what Tolstoy does in *War and Peace.*

In any case, I would characterize the first half of the David story—I am going to be a little more precise than I was when I threw out this phrase in the introduction to my book—as what I have called the first full length portrait of a Machiavellian prince in Western literature. That is, it is a story about a man, to begin with a very young man, who has the wherewithal to gain power, who is verbally and practically resourceful, has military gifts, has musical gifts, and is an utter charmer. Again and again, we are told about the young David that people loved him—the people loved him, Jonathan loved him, Michal the daughter of Saul loved him. Interestingly, it is never the other way around. This is quite consistent; you can never find David as the subject of the verb "to love," rather than its object.

So, we have a man who is on his way to the throne, and is prepared to do what is necessary to get to the throne and then to sit solidly on the throne, which is partly what I mean about a portrait of a Machiavellian prince. Now for me, one quite instructive way that you can see this Machiavellianism played out in the narrative presentation is that in the entire first half of the story until the great pivot, there is never an inside view of David. Well, some of you might say, inside views in the Bible? This isn't exactly Henry James, or Flaubert, or James Joyce, so what am I talking about? In fact, you do have plenty of inside views of characters in the Bible. Sometimes it is a matter of describing what a character feels, or why one character does something, just in a terse narrator's report: and so and so loved so and so, or so and so hated or feared so and so. You also get interior monologue. You might think that this is the sort of term that you might use for a writer such as Virginia Woolf but not for the ancient Hebrew writers. In fact, there are frequent occurrences of interior monologue in biblical narrative but always on a very small scale; that is, you will have quoted speech, which is the speech that the character speaks to itself. But we never get anything like that with David. Now, there is another way in which characters can reveal themselves; that is, the words they speak to others. But then it depends—what is the situation in which they speak those words? And it is quite consistent that through the whole first half of the David story, every single speech of his is in a public setting, and in a public setting when what he says might well serve his political ends, so that one is never quite sure what is behind David's words.

Let me offer one illustration in rapid summary. After David's great success following the killing of Goliath, when David becomes a military captain and the women sing "Saul has struck down his thousands and David his tens of thousands," we are told that all the people loved David, according to this pattern that I just indicated, and that Saul feared David. Then Saul hits on a plan to get rid of David, whom he now has come to see as his dangerous rival. And we have the following: "And Saul had thought: 'Let not my hand be against him, let the hand of the Philistines be against him'" (1 Samuel 18:17).

Now you see this is a perfectly good instance of interior monologue. In this same episode, there are three such snippets of interior monologue assigned to Saul. That is, Saul who is attempting to hatch a scheme against David, is totally transparent to the reader or, in the ancient setting, to the audience. I even have a sneaking suspicion that his transparency—that is, the transparency as rendered through the means of narrative presentation, the interior monologue—might be read as a kind of symptom of the fact that he is not a Machiavellian prince. That is, as a figure of the political realm, he is too readable, too legible, to be able to hang on to power.

What is the role that David plays in this episode? When Saul offers the hand of his daughter to him, David says, "Who am I and who are my kin, my father's clan in Israel, that I should be the king's son-in-law?" Well, what is behind these words? The short answer is that we don't know. But, there are three possibilities. One possibility is court etiquette. The king offers you his daughter: you may be absolutely delighted by the prospect, but deference requires you to say, 'who am I and who are my kin,' and so forth. The second possibility is that David the farm boy from Bethlehem is truly struck with wonder and overwhelmed with modesty by this extravagant offer on the part of King Saul. That reading is conceivable, although I think that that is probably the least likely of my three possibilities. The third possibility is that David has his own political aims steadily in view, and he wants to keep them concealed from Saul. We should keep in mind that David, unbeknownst to Saul, has already been clandestinely anointed as king, in other words as Saul's successor, by the prophet Samuel. This is an anointing that David wants to bring to fruition by taking over the throne when the opportunity presents itself. So he is interested, keenly interested, in marrying Saul's daughter, and we see the ramifications of this much later in the story when he insists that Michal the daughter of Saul be sent back to him after their long separation as a condition for his making peace with the northern tribes loyal to Saul's heirs. He is very interested in marrying her because this connection is going to shore up his claim to the throne. As her husband, he would not be just any Bethlehemite who says I want to be king after Saul, but someone allied by marriage to the incumbent monarch.

Now, if that is the case, he does not want to tip his hand to Saul. Instead of, saying, 'Oh yes I have found favor in your eyes, my liege, and I rejoice in this match you have been so kind as to proffer,' he says, "Who am I and who are my kin, my father's clan in Israel, that I should be the king's son-in-law?" This little instance is consistent with the strategy for presenting David's speech and actions throughout the whole first half of the story, the first panel of this big diptych that makes up the narrative. Let me briefly cite another further instance. When Saul has started pursuing David, Jonathan meets with David, and we encounter an odd and instructively asymmetrical dialogue between the two friends. The narrator introduces David's speech (the beginning of 1 Samuel 20) in the following terms, "And David fled from Naioth in Ramah and came and said before Jonathan." Now that preposition "before" is strange, because in biblical Hebrew, as in modern English, when somebody says something to somebody else, you use the preposition "to," the Hebrew *el*, and not *lifney*, "before." But *lifney*, "before," is the preposition you would use in speaking to some sort of authority, in an address to a king or a prince or perhaps a deity. And then, if you look carefully at that speech, it is very much a speech, a beautifully contrived piece of rhetoric, in which David presents a kind of public articulation of his innocence. So again, you don't know whether he is speaking as a bosom friend to Jonathan (and Jonathan certainly speaks to him in that tone) or whether he is using Jonathan as a kind of sounding board to make a statement that will serve him politically.

Let me quickly add another element to the mix before we go on to a reading of the pivotal episode. One thing you want to pay attention to in the first panel of the diptych is how David responds to the death of people associated with the house of Saul. The one adjective that best qualifies his sundry responses is "eloquent." And the eloquence serves his political purpose. Let me give you the two crucial instances. Saul and Jonathan have both fallen in the battle against the Philistines on Mount Gilboa—David, I should hasten to say, has not been present in the battle. In fact, David has been a Philistine vassal. But the narrative manages to remove him from the scene of battle so that he does not have to fight on the Philistine side. And of course when the word is brought to him, he says, in the King James Version, "How are the mighty fallen," and so forth, delivering his great elegy over Saul and Jonathan, which moving as it is, also positions him politically. He says, in effect: 'Do not think that I had anything to do with this. Do not think of me as an ally of the Philistines. This is a heartfelt loss.' Well maybe it is, one never knows; this is, after all, an unfathomable character. But even as the expression of a heartfelt loss, it also serves a political end.

Still more pointedly in political terms—and this will be my last example of the hidden David before we move to the pivot and then the revelation of the private David—after several years of a bitter civil war between the house of David and the house of Saul following Saul's death, Saul's general Abner sues for peace with David. And he comes to David's headquarters in Hebron, and they agree on a peace treaty. But when Abner goes off, he is ambushed by his rival, Joab, who is David's military commander, probably for two reasons: because Joab has a vendetta score to pay off against Abner, who has killed Joab's younger brother in battle, and also Joab does not want a competitor for the job of chief field commander of David's forces. When the news is brought to David that Abner has been assassinated, he does two things. He recites a short elegy, or composes and recites a short elegy over Abner: "Like the death of the base/ should Abner have died?/ Your hands—never bound,/ your feet never placed in fetters?/ As one falls before scoundrels you fell" (2 Samuel 3: 33–34). And then he disclaims any responsibility in the death of Abner and delivers a round curse against Joab, and he undertakes a very public rite of mourning. The very last words of this episode are spoken by David to the people: "And I am gentle, and just anointed king, and these sons of Zeruiah are too hard for me. May the LORD pay back the evildoer according to his evil!" (Zeruiah is the mother of Joab and his brother Abishai, and the two of them emerge in the story as mafiosi types who happen to be David's nephews. Zeruiah is his sister, a fact that seems to determine the rare identification of the characters by a matronymic instead of a patronymic. David's military base of support starts off as a kind of family militia, if you want to think of it in concrete political terms.) Are we to take David's expression of abhorrence over the murder of Abner and his helplessness before the sons of Zeruiah at face value? It is very hard to evaluate. Perhaps he really is too "gentle" and too inexperienced in the challenges of ruling to be able to cope with these implacable nephews of his. There is a good deal in the subsequent narrative, especially during David's later years, that would appear to confirm the claim he makes here. But we should also observe that it certainly serves his interest to push off the responsibility for any death of someone associated with the house of Saul onto somebody else. Given the public occasion of David's utterance, as throughout the first half of his story, we cannot be sure whether he is truly anguished over the killing of the man with whom he was about to make peace and caught up in a power struggle with his own henchmen, or whether he is relieved to have him out of the way.

All these questions, then, mark David as a kind of occluded figure, a character whose motives and inner states remain hidden up to the middle of the story. And the middle of the story is as follows: David has now conquered Jerusalem from the Jebusites, which is a very shrewd way of consolidating his dynasty, because being a Jebusite town, it does not belong to any of the tribes, so it can be something like Washington D.C., not owing allegiance to any one regional group, and because he can claim in setting up his capital there that he is king of all the tribes together, not just of the tribe of Judah or the two southern tribes. With his monarchy consolidated, he sends Joab at the head of an expeditionary force across to Jordan to fight against the Ammonites at Rabbath-Ammon, which is roughly where Amman is today in the Hashemite kingdom of Jordan. And then we encounter the famous story of David and Bathsheba, which is the pivot to which I alluded. Now everybody thinks with good warrant that this is a story about adultery, but it is also a story about politics and political institutions; and that is what I would like to highlight. For this reason, I will read a bit of it in my translation and comment: "And it happened at the turn of the year, at the time the kings sally forth, that David sent out Joab and his servants with him in all Israel, and they ravaged the Ammonites and besieged Rabbah. And David was sitting in Jerusalem" (2 Samuel 11: 1).

The time when the kings go out is probably the spring when winter rains stop; it is roughly the same kind of climate as California, and so you can maneuver with the troops once it is sufficiently dry. There is a famous pun here, what I think is really an orthographic pun, and I would like to discuss that for a moment. The Hebrew word for kings is *melakhim,* which is spelled with the three Hebrew consonants *mem, lamed,* and *kaf.* The Masoretic Text—the received text in Hebrew—spells it in a different way, although from our own distance we cannot be very sure about the difference in pronunciation in the ancient period. The received text spells the word for "kings" here with an extra consonant, an *aleph,* which would make it *mala'khim* instead of *melakhim.* (At the same time, a marginal note in the Masoretic Text directs us to pronounce it as though it were written without the additional *aleph.*) Now, *mala'khim* means messengers. And I think that there is a play between those two terms; that is, messengers is a key term for the whole story, as I will try to show in a moment, and there is almost a sort of substitution of messenger for king, or a way in which the king becomes dependent on the messenger.

The other word I want to pick up here is "sitting." I decided to translate it quite literally, *wedawid yoshev biyushalayim*—"and David was sitting in Jerusalem." Of course, it also obviously means staying or dwelling. But I think we want to capture the literal sense of sitting. You might remember that the word "sedentary" comes from the Latin word that means "to sit." And David, who has been a military hero, and has built up a little empire, is now seen as a sedentary monarch. Very quickly, as the story unfolds, we will see what the consequences of that condition are, because at least in part his being a sedentary monarch is what gets him into trouble.

Let me go on with the text: "And it happened at eventide that David arose from his bed and walked about on the roof of the king's house, and he saw from the roof a woman bathing, and the woman was very beautiful. And David sent, and inquired after the woman, and the one he sent said, 'Why, this is Bathsheba daughter of Eliam wife of Uriah the Hittite.'" Now there is something a little peculiar here. Jerusalem was not a big town around the year 1000 before the Christian era. David's palace—there is no specialized word for palace; it is simply referred to as the king's house—overlooks Bathsheba's house; she's his down-the-hill neighbor. If this same Eliam is one of his elite fighting corps, then she is a daughter of one of his inner circle of warriors, and yet he seems never to have heard of her. He does not know who she is, what her name is, who her father is, whether she has a husband or who her husband might be, all of which suggests something about his sedentary rule to begin with—that he is out of touch. He does not know what is going on right around him. One thing that has inevitably occurred is that once the monarchy was consolidated as an institution (and I think this is pretty close to the surface of the story), there was an inescapable need to create a royal bureaucracy. That is, you have to have intermediaries interposing themselves between the king and his subjects. And while this story is certainly about lust, it is also all about intermediaries, and hence there are two words, one a noun and one a verb, that keep coming back again and again. The noun is *mala'kh*, "messenger," and the verb is *lishloah*, "to send," which is what you do with a messenger.

Let us listen to those crucial words as they mark the story: "And David sent messengers and fetched her and she came to him and he lay with her, she having just cleansed herself of her impurity, and she returned to her house. And the woman became pregnant and sent and told David and said, 'I am pregnant.' And David sent (again that key verb) to Joab: 'Send me Uriah the Hittite.' And Joab sent Uriah the Hittite to David." By the way, the three words, "I am pregnant," are two words in the Hebrew, and are the only words that Bathsheba speaks in this whole episode. It is quite amazing.

When she returns to the narrative just before David's death, however, she has a lot to say, so maybe she has changed over the course of time. I also have certain suspicions about the degree to which she might have been complicit in this act of adultery (certainly later on, she shows herself to be a woman with her eye on the main chance), but that is going to take me a little aside of what I want to talk about.

A note about translation: You heard perhaps almost to the point of awkwardness how the writer contrives to repeat, "And David sent…, And David sent…, the woman…sent,…Send me…and Joab sent Uriah." Now many modern translators have concluded that such repetition does not sound good in English, so they use an abundance of synonyms for the sake of a more 'elegant' variation. I think this is a fatal mistake, because biblical narrative highlights its meaning by repeating key words. In this instance, we need to be reminded repeatedly that this is a story that is all about sending and about messengers. Now, it would take too long to read through the entire story, but what I want to do is to refer to it in summary. Most of the details will be familiar, but I'd like to read it with a particular focus on this issue of agency. Another way you could translate the key term *mala'kh*, messenger, is "agent."

David sends to the battlefield, to the front, to bring Uriah back. Now, he does not say why, although that in itself might arouse certain suspicions, and Joab, the recipient of David's message, is after all a very canny character. What happens next is well known: Uriah returns and comes to David, and David encourages him to go down to his house. What David wants is a cover-up for the illegitimate conception. (The seemingly casual detail in the initial part of the story—"she having just cleansed herself of her impurity"— refers to the prescribed ritual bath after menstruation, so we know that she could not possibly be pregnant by her husband. As the story evolves, this becomes an important narrative datum.) David's scheme, then, is to get the husband to go down to his house and sleep with his wife; then she can pass the child off as her husband's rather than David's. Instead, Uriah refuses to go down, and he delivers a speech in which he figures as the exemplary Israelite good soldier even though he is Hittite in origin: "The Ark and Israel and Judah are sitting in huts, and my master Joab and my master's servants are encamped in the open field, and shall I then come to my house to eat and to drink and to lie with my wife?" It is noteworthy that the crucial purpose that David had in mind, to have Uriah sleep with his wife, is precisely what he took pains not to mention when he urged Uriah to go to his house, but Uriah himself now strategically adds the missing element.

There are two ways to read this confrontation between the adulterous king and the good soldier, and a long time ago, two very bright Israeli literary scholars proposed that the story is deliberately contrived to be read in two ways. Either Uriah knows that David has slept with his wife, in which case he is playing a very dangerous game of sticking it to the king, being the conscience of the king ('how could I do this after the troops are out in the field, and go down to do all these things and lie with my wife'), or he does not know, in which case Uriah serves as the vehicle of dramatic irony. David tries to persuade him twice, but Uriah is adamant in his refusal to go down to his house. The king even tries to get him drunk, and that, too, is of no avail, so then he "sends"—again that crucial verb—a message to Uriah's commander. Presumably the message would have been sealed with the king's seal or wrapped with a little thong and would be written on a small papyrus or parchment scroll. The message, which the good soldier is supposed to bring back to the front, is to Joab. And the gist of David's message is as follows: 'I want you to approach the wall of Rabbath-Ammon which you are besieging, and then suddenly pull back, leaving Uriah all by himself, and let him be killed.' David's strategy now seems to be that if he can't have the cover story, he will try to get rid of the husband and then marry the wife very quickly and claim, perhaps, that it is a seven-month pregnancy.

What happens in the rest of the story is that messages are sent through agents, but the messages keep getting distorted. This of course is what is bound to happen, for any sending of messages when one is dependent on the intermediary turns out to be something like the old game of telephone. In this case, Joab is too shrewd to follow out David's orders literally, because if he did, it would be quite transparent that David wanted Uriah killed. So, quite unblinkingly, Joab makes a decision that not only Uriah has to die but other men have to die as well. Accordingly, he sends a whole contingent of his soldiers up to the wall, and many of them are cut down by the archers shooting down from the walls; and among those cut down, is Uriah the Hittite. At this point, after the murder by proxy of Uriah, another problem with message-sending arises, which is that Joab has to send back a discrete but effective message to David telling him what happened. This time the message is an oral communication. Joab makes a point of telling the messenger that, should the king express anger that the men were sent so close to the wall of the city and thus exposed to the archers, he should inform David that, "Your servant Uriah the Hittite also died." The messenger quickly concludes—Could it be that Joab actually wanted him to draw this conclusion?—that this is exactly what David wants to hear, and he does not want to run the risk of David's wrath.

David has, after all, killed messengers bearing ill tidings earlier in the story. So instead of following the precise order of Joab's instructions, the messenger rushes into David and tells him the whole story, making sure to add, before the king has a chance to react, "and your servant Uriah the Hittite also died." David, far from showing anger or remorse, responds with odd equanimity, saying, in words intended to be carried back to Joab, "Let this thing not seem evil in your eyes, for the sword consumes sometimes one way sometimes another." This sounds like an ancient Hebrew equivalent of the First World War adage, 'every bullet had its billet,' that is to say, people die in battle, so what can I do? Thus, David emerges from all this seeing quite callous.

What we have then, is a whole network of people implicated in this story of adultery and murder, finding out about the story, and manipulating the story in different ways, even as David tries to effect a cover-up. And this is part of what I had in mind when I noted that this is a story about the institutionalization of the monarchy and what happens when a king is compelled to work through the agency of others. But now let us proceed directly to the fateful climax of the whole pivotal episode. Nathan the prophet then comes to David and denounces him. He begins with rhetorical cunning by delivering the famous parable of the poor-man's ewe. When David, not guessing Nathan's purpose, listens to the parable—this works very much like the play within the play in *Hamlet*—it proves to be something to catch the conscience of the king. Outraged by what he has heard, David pronounces a death sentence, "Doomed to death is the man who has done this thing." Then Nathan memorably says, "You are the man." And he follows this immediately with an astonishing speech, which is a rather blood-curdling curse on the house of David. And part of the profundity of this narrative—as a narrative about the founding of the Davidic dynasty—is that it is also a story about the fall of the house of David, from the very beginning. The reader of the David story who perhaps understood this best is William Faulkner, in *Absalom Absalom!*, where his David figure, Thomas Sutpen, aspires to found a grand dynasty in the slave-holding South, and the abject failure of his project turns out to be a story about the fall of the house of Sutpen.

The curse will begin to work itself out immediately and then will dominate much of the rest of the story of David as we see him progressively losing power till, at the very end, we find him totally powerless, literally and figuratively impotent, lying on his death bed. But the first manifestation of Nathan's curse is that the infant born by Bathsheba of her adulterous intercourse with David, is born deathly sick. For seven days and nights, David lies on the ground, refuses to eat and drink (these acts by the way are very much like the ones that Uriah undertook at the palace gate)—conventional gestures of mourning but in this case undertaken as supplication to God. David hopes that God will listen and have mercy on the child. This, by the way, is the first of several sons that David will lose in the course of the story, and as readers we are invited to compare the various scenes of mourning. When the child dies on the seventh day, David sees his courtiers whispering to one another, and he realizes what has happened. Let us attend to the language of the story at this crucial juncture:

> And it happened on the seventh day that the child died, and David's servants were afraid to tell him that the child was dead, for they said, "Look, while the child was alive, we spoke to him and he did not heed our voice, and how can we say to him, the child is dead? He will do some harm." And David saw that his servants were whispering to each other and David understood that the child was dead. And David said to his servants, "Is the child dead?" And they said, "He is dead." (2 Samuel 12:17–19)

Here I want to observe how, like all great writers, the author of this story makes a virtue of an idiomatic necessity of his own language. Biblical Hebrew, like Latin, is one of those languages in which there is no word for yes. That is, if you want to answer a question in the affirmative, you answer by repeating the most significant term of the question. So, in biblical Hebrew, if you were to ask me, "Have you eaten?", instead of saying "Yes," I would say, "I have eaten." So here we have "dead," "dead," "dead," like a drumbeat in the story. As in English, this is a monosyllabic word, *meit* in the Hebrew, and the courtiers' response that I have translated as "He is dead" is actually just the bleak syllable, *meit*, "dead." But to continue:

> And David rose from the ground and bathed and rubbed himself with oil and changed his garments and came into the house of the Lord and worshiped and came back to his house and asked that food be set out for him, and he ate. And his servants said him, "What is this thing that you have done? For the sake of the living child you fasted and wept, and when the child was dead, you arose and ate food? (2 Samuel 12: 20–21)

Now this is puzzling, it is paradoxical, and I would suggest, perhaps parenthetically but more than parenthetically, that one of the measures of the profundity of the David story as the representation of a human life is that this human life is so unpredictable, that it keeps turning and twisting in surprising ways. To borrow a wonderful formula of the British novelist Elizabeth Bowen: "Characters in a novel should be unpredictable before the fact and inevitable afterwards." And I think this is quite true of David, who moves from being hidden to self-revelation, from self-affirmation to self-abasement, right through to the end of the story when, on his deathbed, he is implacable about enemies whom he has previously forgiven.

But, what I would like to do now in concluding is briefly to attend closely to the tenor of David's words when he responds to the question of his courtiers. As we have just heard, they ask him in bafflement, 'Why is it that you now when the child is dead, arise and eat food?' "And he said: 'While the child was still alive I fasted and wept, for I thought, who knows, the Lord may favor me and the child will live. And now that he is dead, why should I fast? Can I bring him back again? I am going to him and he will not come back to me.'"

Now, against the background of all the David speeches in the first half of the story, this is quite breathtaking. It is something, I think, totally new. Even though the occasion is a public one, and he is surrounded by his courtiers, it is hard to infer any kind of political purpose in this speech. And from a certain point of view, you might say that it is not an eloquent speech. It exhibits, of course, another order of eloquence, but it is not elegy; it is not a piece of speechmaking rhetoric of the sort we have seen him deftly execute time after time in the first half of the story. Yet, it is a very naked and moving statement, 'And now that he is dead why should I fast? Can I bring him back again? I am going to him, and he will not come back to me.' This, the last note, is I think worth listening to closely because it is not only very moving in itself, but it gives us a clue to the second panel of the diptych, to the second half of the David story. What is he saying, and why is he saying it?

There is no calculation of ambition and power here, or anything of the sort. The king is faced with the bleak fact of his child's death. The first thing he says about it is that it is irrevocable: 'I can't bring him back.' The second thing he confesses is that this inexorability of death makes him confront his own mortality. Like King Lear, the glorious King David is reduced to a "bare forked thing," exposed to the harshness of an indifferent Nature. Beyond the elaborate games of power that he has been playing, David grimly recognizes that he is a mortal like everyone else: "I am going to him and he will not come back to me." In the second half of the story, what we will see is David in his mortal frailty, David in his vulnerability, vulnerable to the power-brokers around him, vulnerable to his own children, and in still another great moment, the one that I think we all remember, in which he is bereaved of his son, anguished by the conflict between his role as king, his role in the realm of politics, which dictates that he be the firm enemy of his son Absalom, and his other role, his role as a father. This intolerable conflict emerges, or at least one side of the conflict emerges, in that tremendous stutter of grief, "Absalom Absalom, my son, my son. Would that I had died in your stead!" The greatness of this story, then, is its unflagging ability to show us not only the complex machinery of politics and how political institutions affect individual character, and vice versa, but also the human imperfections and the ineluctable limitations of the human condition of those caught up in the political realm.

ROBERT ALTER
University of California at Berkeley

NOTES

1. From Robert Alter, trans. and comm., *The David Story; A Translation and Commentary of 1 and 2 Samuel* (New York and London: W. W. Norton, 1999), ix.

2. Erich Auerbach, *Mimesis: The Representation of Reality in Western Literature,* trans. Willard R. Trask (Princeton: Princeton University Press, 1953).

RECENT TRANSLATIONS OF DAVID

Alter, Robert. *The David Story.* New York: W. W. Norton, 1999.

Fox, Everett. *Give Us a King! Samuel, Saul, and David.* New York: Schocken, 1999.

McCarthy, P. Kyle, Jr. *The Anchor Bible: I and 2 Samuel.* 2 vols. New York: Doubleday, 1980, 1984.

SUGGESTIONS FOR FURTHER READING

Avramsky, Shmuel. in *The World of the Bible: 2 Samuel* (in Hebrew). Tel Aviv: Revivim, 1989.

Bar-Efrat, Shimon. *1 and 2 Samuel: With Introduction and Commentary* (in Hebrew). Tel Aviv: Am Oved, 1996.

Faulkner, William. *Absalom, Absalom!* New York: Vintage Books, 1990.

Fokkelman, J. P. *Narrative Art and Poetry in the Books of Samuel.* 3 vols. Assen: Van Gorcum, 1981–1990.

Garsiel, Moshe. In *The World of the Bible: 1 and 2 Samuel.* 2 vols. (in Hebrew). Tel Aviv: Revivim, 1984, 1989.

Gevaryabu, Haim. In *The World of the Bible: I Samuel* (in Hebrew). Tel Aviv: Revivim, 1984.

Perry, Menahem, and Sternberg, Meir. "The King through Ironic Eyes" (in Hebrew). *Hasifrut* I (1968): 263–292.

Polzin, Robert. *David and the Deuteronomist.* Bloomington: Indiana University Press, 1993.

——. *Samuel and the Deuteronomist.* Bloomington: Indiana University Press, 1989.

von Rad, Gerhard. "The Beginnings of History Writing in Ancient Israel." In *The Problem of the Hexateuch and Other Essays.* Trans. E. W. Trueman Dicken. New York: McGraw-Hill, 1955.

Rost, Leonhard. Die *Ueberlieferung von der Thronnachfolge Davids.* Stuttgart: W. Kohlhammer, 1926.

Shalev, Meir. *The Bible Now* (in Hebrew). Jerusalem: Schocken, 1985.

Shklovsky, Viktor. "Art as Technique." In *Russian Formalist Criticism.* Ed. L. T. Lemon and M. J. Reis. Lincoln: University of Nebraska Press, 1965.

Speiser, E. A. *The Anchor Bible: Genesis.* Garden City, N.Y.: Doubleday, 1964.

Sternberg, Meir. *The Poetics of Biblical Narrative.* Bloomington: Indiana University Press, 1985.

Yadin, Yigal. *The Art of Warfare in Biblical Lands.* 2 vols. New York: McGraw-Hill, 1963.

DISCUSSION QUESTIONS

How is kingship viewed as an institution in this narrative? Keeping in mind the crucial literary distinction between the views of author and character, what are we meant to conclude about the judiciousness of Israel's decision to have a king?

The story of David may well have been the work of an adept writer working within a larger tradition of biblical story-telling. Note the use, for example, of biblical type-scenes (e.g., 1 Sam. 2), framing scenes (e.g., 1 Sam. 4 and 2 Sam. 18), and intertextual echoes between one biblical episode and another (e.g., Gen. 34 and 2 Sam. 13). How do such narrative conventions function within the overall narrative framework?

How would you explain Saul's eventual loss of favor from Samuel and, apparently, from God? Is he responsible for his gradual demise in the story or a victim of circumstance? Do you take him to be a sympathetic figure or a fool? How would you explain Samuel's eventual repudiation of Saul and Saul's eventual repudiation of David?

What is it about the young David that at first so recommends him to Saul above David's older brothers and other possible claimants to the throne? How would you explain Jonathan's loyalty to David and David's to Jonathan?

David has at least two memorable opportunities in the story to do away with his persecutor Saul—in the cave in En-gedi and at Saul's camp in the wilderness of Ziph. Why doesn't he?

What does the famous story of David and Bathsheba reflect about the character of David and his rule as king? What are the psychological and narrative implications of this episode?

We first encounter Bathsheba in the story as an object of King David's lust and later as a shrewd political strategist on behalf of her son. What might we deduce about the character of Bathsheba from the brief but suggestive details we are given?

What is the fuller possible significance of David's lament for his deceased child—"I am going to him and he will not come back to me" (2 Sam. 12.23)?

What are the roots of Absalom's apostasy and conspiracy? What is the nature of David's response?

How do David's various speeches and public utterances bear upon his larger political strategies and ambitions?

What is the literary role played by God in this narrative? What is the nature of his covenant with Samuel, with Saul, with David? How does he make his wishes known? Are his motives clear? Are his expectations fair?

Discussion Points

• The story of Samuel and its narrative and stylistic relationship to the stories of previous prophets and patriarchs.

• Style of presentation, narrative significance, and textual inconsistencies in the story of David and Goliath.

• The relationship between David and his several wives: Michal, Abigail, Bathsheba.

• The role of the prophets (e.g., Samuel, Nathan) and priests (e.g., Ahimelech, Abiathar, Zadok) in the narrative, and their relationship to political figures (e.g., Saul and David).

• Literary and psychological significance of the rape of Tamar.

• The role and treatment of messengers in the narrative.

• Style and significance of scenes of mourning in the story.

• Death scenes—of Saul, of Abner, of Absalom, of David.

Points for Further Investigation

• Religious significance of the Ark of the Covenant throughout the story and the narrative significance of 1 Sam. 5-7.

• Origin and meaning of the prophetic "ecstasies" displayed on occasion by Saul, David, and prophets.

• How the events of the story reflect the actual topography, climate, seasons, or geography of ancient Israel?

• The literary structure, style, and authorship of the David story in relation to other ancient biblical books.

• The significance and background of Saul's audience with the "ghostwife" or female necromancer of Endor?

• The role and religious or political significance of marked physical beauty (e.g., of David, of Bathsheba, of Absalom) in this narrative.

• David as poet, dancer, singer, and psalmist.

• The theology of David and its relationship to the Ark of the Covenant, the people of Israel, and the prophets.

ODYSSEY

There is a certain literary, not to say chronological, justice in assigning an essay on Homer's great epic, the *Odyssey*, to the central place of this collection. Here the gifted contemporary translator, Stanley Lombardo, leads us masterfully to the poetic heart of Homer's artistic vision—the creative inner light in which the poet conceived and the hearer realizes the famous story of Odysseus's return journey after his participation in the Trojan War. For generations, scholars have struggled to explain the origins of this remarkable work. We are relatively confident that Homer, the blind bard of tradition, lived in the eight century B.C.E., probably in Asia Minor; that he stood at the acme and the end of a highly sophisticated tradition of oral story-telling; that the two great epics associated with his name, the *Iliad* and the *Odyssey*, were written down sometime in the late eighth or seventh century B.C.E. But here any consensus begins to break down. Was Homer a single author who composed both epic poems or is the name only a placeholder of sorts for an entire tradition of otherwise anonymous storytellers whose oral performances culminated in these two great works? Whatever the case may be, in his powerfully compelling translation of the *Odyssey*, and the suggestive essay that follows, Lombardo conceives Homer's narrative—from Odysseus's hair-raising encounter with the Cyclops to his long-awaited return to Ithaca—as the realization of a single mind and the expression of a single, moving poetic voice.

ODYSSEY TIMELINE

1600		Height of Mycenaean civilization
1225		Fall of Troy
1000		Sea raids, migrations, Mycenaean collapse
850		Beginning of Greek renaissance
775		Earliest Greek alphabetic writing
735		Homeric composition of *Iliad*
725		Homeric composition of *Odyssey*
6–4c		Copies circulate throughout Greek world
3c	B.C.E.	Alexandrian scholars create standard edition
	C.E.	
2–5c		Parchment codex replaces papyrus scroll
14c		Re-introduction of *Odyssey* into Italy
1453		Fall of Byzantium
1868		Schliemann explores Homeric Ithaka
1870–1873		Schliemann's excavations at Troy
1930's		Systematic British excavations on Ithaca
1980's		Odyssey Project of the Greek Archaeological Service

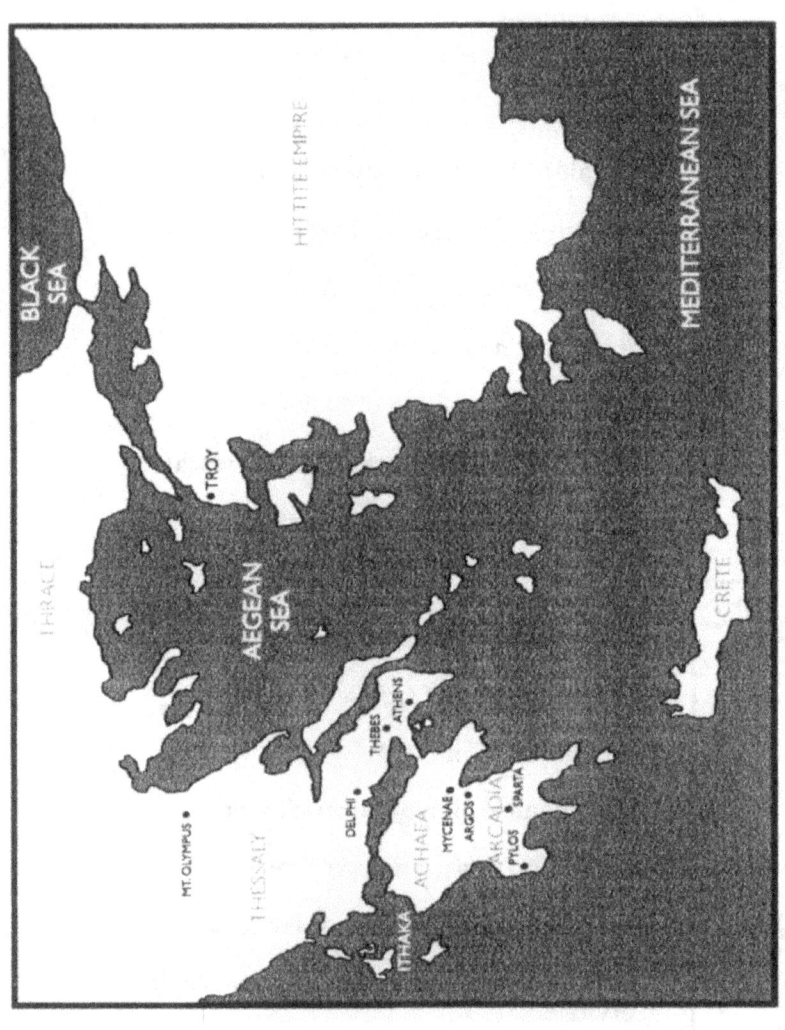

ANCIENT MEDITERRANEAN

HOMER'S LIGHT

Speak, Memory—
    Of the cunning hero,
The wanderer, blown off course time and again
After he plundered Troy's sacred heights.
    Speak,
Of all the cities he saw, the minds he grasped,
The suffering deep in his heart at sea
As he struggled to survive and bring his men home
But could not save them, hard as he tried—
The fools—destroyed by their own recklessness
When they ate the oxen of Hyperion the Sun,
And that god snuffed out their day of return.   I.10
        Of all these things,
Speak, Immortal One,
And tell the tale once more in our time.

As a translator my main concern has been to find a voice for Homer in English, to remember my own voice as Homer's and to merge it with his. This is something I have tried to do, without any success at all for decades, since I first encountered Homer in Greek as an undergraduate at Loyola University in New Orleans. Poetry had already become the stream of my life, but here was an immortal river of poetry. What first impressed me was the sound of his Greek verse, and it was immediately apparent to me that the *sound* of Homer's voice in Greek cannot be found in English. If you listen to the first ten lines of Homer's *Odyssey* you can hear for yourself a kind of music, a sheer physical beauty, that cannot be heard in English.

As the critic Donald Carne-Ross has observed, a translator doesn't have a hope in hell of taking on Homer at the level of verbal music. But other essential qualities of Homer's voice can perhaps be heard in English—his directness, simplicity, immediacy, his deep humanity. These are qualities in Homer's poetry that I became familiar with over time, through long listening. They are really qualities of mind. So finding Homer's voice has become for me finding his mind.

What this has been like for me I can best express in terms of a classical form of Zen meditation known as *kong-an* practice that I have been deeply involved with first as student and then as teacher for the past twenty odd years. *Kong-an* practice directs our attention to the mind before words and speech appear. The great Sung Dynasty master, Wu Men, who compiled the first classic collection of *kong-ans*, tells us that if we do this practice, we can lock eyebrows with the masters of old, seeing through their eyes and hearing with their ears. Who would not like to do that?[1]

Kong-ans are an aspect of formal Zen training in which the student, in a face to face interview with a teacher, tries to attain the mind of the teacher and of the great teachers in his lineage. Here is an example:

> A monk asked Un Mun, 'What is speech that goes beyond Buddha and the patriarchs?' Un Mun answered, 'Cake.'

The point of working with this *kong-an* is to grasp Un Mun's mind the moment before he said 'cake,' and to present that mind clearly and directly. Then there is no teacher, no student, only the original mind that we all share. Here is another *kong-an*, a very simple one. This stick, this sound, and your mind, are they the same or different? How can you answer?

Homer has always been one of my teachers, and I realized after I had been doing *kong-an* practice for about ten years that my approach to translation was changing, that I was beginning to go beyond the words, beyond language and style, to the mind that produced them. This made all the difference. I had been trying most of my life to lock eyebrows with Homer, trying to attain the mind of the great master of European poetry, and now that mind, and the voice, was beginning to appear.

Who was he? We know so little about him. "A blind man who lives on rugged Chios" is as much as we are told (this almost an aside at the end of the Homeric "Hymn to Delian Apollo"). Some modern scholars have suggested that we should think of "Homer" more as a tradition of epic poetry than an individual composer, but for me there is one mind that runs through both the *Iliad* and *Odyssey*, one poet at their deep conception—and I can well believe that this poet was blind. Jacques Lusseyran, the French resistance leader, tells us that a few months after he lost his eyesight as a young boy he found that the whole world was filled with light, and that the light came from his mind and was the core of his being. This passage from his autobiography, *And There Was Light*, which describes how he gained a power of inward vision, strikes me as a wonderful expression of how Homer's mind works, peopling a universe and illuminating everything within it:

> At this point some instinct...made me change my course. I began to look more closely, not at things but at a world closer to myself, looking from an inner a place

to one further within, instead of clinging to the movement of sight toward the world outside. Immediately, the substance of the universe drew together, redefined and peopled itself anew. I was aware of a radiance emanating from a place I knew nothing about, a place which might as well have been outside me as within. But radiance was there, or, to put it more precisely, light.... I could no more have denied it than people with eyes can deny that they see. I was not light myself, I knew that, but I bathed in it as element which blindness had suddenly brought much closer. I could feel light rising, spreading, resting on objects, giving them form, then leaving them.[2]

Homer's mind, too, and his world, are filled with light that rises, spreads, rests on things and on people and gives them form. Light is the esthetic expression of the poet's mind. In the *Iliad* the light is intense, the light of noon, searing and white, the light of Zeus, whose very name means the sky's brightness, illuminating mortal heroes in their hour of glory. Here is Hector in that light:

> And Hector needed no urging. Hector XV.636
> Raged like the War God, the Spear Wielder
> *Fire that consumes a wooded mountainside,*
> Foam flecking his mouth, eyes burning
> Under fierce brows, and the helmet
> Encasing his face a sinister glitter 640
> As Hector fought, as Zeus himself
> Shed a cone of light from the aether
> Around the solitary warrior, but only
> For this brief moment.

And here is Achilles:

> *Snow flurries can come so thick and fast*
> *From the cold northern sky that the wind* XIX.380
> *That bears them becomes an icy, blinding glare.*
> So too the gleaming, polished weaponry—
> The helmets, shields, spears, and plated corselets—
> All the bronze paraphernalia of war
> That issued from the ships. The rising glare
> Reflected off the coppery sky, and the land beneath
> Laughed under the arcing metallic glow.
> A deep bass thrumming rose from the marching feet.
> And, like a bronze bolt in the center, Achilles,
> Who now began to arm. 390
>   His eyes glowed
> Like white-hot steel, and he gritted his teeth
> Against the grief that had sunk into his bones,
> And every motion he made in putting on the armor

> Forged for him in heaven was an act of passion
> Directed against the Trojans: clasping on his shins
> The greaves trimmed in silver at the ankles,
> Strapping the corselet onto his chest, slinging
> The silver-studded bronze sword around a shoulder,
> And then lifting the massive, heavy shield
> That spilled light around it as if it were the moon.   400
>
> *Or a fire that has flared up in a lonely settlement*
> *High in the hills of an island, reflecting light*
> *On the faces of men who have put out to sea*
> *And must watch helplessly as rising winds*
> *Bear them away from their dear ones.*
>
> So too the terrible beauty of Achilles' shield,
> A fire in the sky.

In the *Odyssey* we see by a softer light, the rose-light of dawn, the firelight in a room. The ancient critic Longinus compares the poet of the *Odyssey* to the setting sun, adding: "The grandeur remains apart from the intensity." Penelope waits and dreams in that quiet light; Telemachus wakes to it; and Odysseus, in the dark of the moon, returns to it and becomes himself again.

The light in the *Odyssey* casts an enchantment over the most ordinary actions in the poem. Here is Penelope making her first appearance in the poem:

> They were sitting hushed in silence, listening
> To the great harper as he sang the tale
> Of the hard journeys home that Pallas Athena
> Ordained for the Greeks on their way back from Troy.   III.345
>
> His song drifted upstairs, and Penelope,
> Wise daughter of Icarius, took it all in.
> She came down the steep stairs of her house—
> Not alone, two maids trailed behind—
> And when she had come among the suitors   350
> She stood shawled in light by a column
> That supported the roof of the great house,
> Hiding her cheeks behind her silky veils.

And here is Telemachus:

> Dawn's pale rose fingers brushed across the sky
> And Odysseus' son got out of bed and dressed.
> He slung his sharp sword around his shoulder,
> Then tied oiled leather sandals onto his feet,
> And walked out of the bedroom like a god.   II.5
> Wasting no time, he ordered the heralds
> To call an assembly. The heralds' cries
> Rang out through the town, and the men
> Gathered quickly, their long hair streaming.

> Telemachus strode along carrying a spear 10
> And accompanied by two lean hounds.
> Athena shed a silver grace upon him,
> And everyone marveled at him as he entered.

Penelope walks across a room, Telemachus gets dressed—and these actions are as magical as any of the marvelous adventures Odysseus has. The great poem, again as Longinus puts it, is like the sea at low tide, withdrawn into its solitude, greatness ebbing and flowing, and the poet wanders along the shore where there are many curious things, and into the mythical and incredible: "What else can we call all this" Longinus asks, "but the dreaming of a Zeus?" But it is not only in the midst of the mythical and incredible—the Sirens, the Island of the Sun, the Underworld, the house of Circe— that we are entranced. Everywhere the poet turns his mind there is a sense of seeing things as if for the first time, and seeing their essential wholeness. "One by one, each thing is complete;/One by one each thing has it," as an old Zen poem puts it. The spell that we are under is an enlightening enchantment, not the drowsiness of the lotus-eaters, who become forgetful of home, but a waking realization that every moment of experience is our luminous, original home. This is the true *nostos*, the true homecoming, of the *Odyssey*, and the completion of the poetic vision that begins in the raw, brilliant radiance of the *Iliad.*

Nostos, "return home"—here is the word in the fourth line of the *Odyssey*— expressing the poem's genre, theme, and direction. And here—in the third line—is the word *noos*, "mind," expressing the essential characteristic of Odysseus, the cunning hero who survives by grasping the minds of others and whose own mind cannot be matched except by Athena and most memorably, by Penelope. Both words originally meant to move from darkness to light. To come to the light, to come to consciousness, is to return home. But how final an experience is this? Homer brings Odysseus home, but his return to Ithaca will not be his last voyage.

When Odysseus visits Teiresias in Hades (*Odyssey* 11. 119 ff.) to learn the route of his voyage home, the Theban prophet tells him of another journey he must make after his eventual return to Ithaca:

> "...when you have slain
> The suitors in your hall, by ruse or by sword,
> Then you must go off again, carrying a broad-bladed oar,
> Until you come to men who know nothing of the sea, XI.120
> Who eat their food unsalted, and have never seen
> Red-prowed ships or oars that wing them along.
> And I will tell you a sure sign that you have found them,
> One you cannot miss. When you meet another traveler

> Who thinks you are carrying a winnowing fan,
> Then you must fix your oar in the earth
> And offer sacrifice to Lord Poseidon,
> A ram, a bull, and a boar in its prime.
> Then return to your home and offer
> Perfect sacrifice to the immortal gods   130
> Who hold high heaven, to each in turn.
> And death will come to you off the sea,
> A death so gentle, and carry you off
> When you are worn out in sleek old age,
> Your people prosperous all around you.
> All this will come true for you as I have told."

Odysseus reports Teiresias' prescription to Penelope in the course of his late-night account of his adventures after the two of them are re-united, but Homer's *Odyssey* ends with its hero still home in Ithaca, where his quest and the ever contracting circles of the great poem have brought him. We are left to assume that at some later time Odysseus made his inland journey as Poseidon's missionary, and having discharged that duty, returned to Ithaca and to Penelope to await the prophesied gentle death from the sea (or far from the sea—the Greek is ambiguous). Teiresias' prophecy of a quiet, domestic ending to Odysseus' life is in perfect accordance with Homer's characterization of the wandering hero. Odysseus never wanted to go to Troy, and when the war was over all he wanted to do was return home. The *Odyssey* is a poem of *nostos*, "return," a centripetal poem, a home-seeking poem. Plato understands Homer's Odysseus well when, in a vision of metempsychosis at the end of the *Republic*, he has the hero select a quiet, domestic life for his next reincarnation.

But even before Plato, there began a tradition of sequels to Homer's *Odyssey*, prompted at least in part by Teiresias' prophecy, that reactivate the man of many turns and lead him to new destinies, taking him away from home in a centrifugal quest for knowledge, experience and meaning—for *noos*. This tradition began in antiquity just a century or two after Homer and culminated in Nikos Kazantzakis' *Odyssey*, a twentieth century mega-poem—it goes far beyond epic—that synthesizes and transcends everything in the sequel tradition (and just about everything an Eastern and Western philosophy and religion as well). I would like to trace the outlines of this tradition picking it up with Dante, and then, when we have seen Odysseus off on his last voyage, return to Homer's *Odyssey* and consider a little more deeply the implications of the two cognate, light-seeking words—*nostos*, "return home," and *noos*, "mind"—that stand at the beginning of Homer's *Odyssey* and are at the heart of his poetry.

The sequels to Homer's *Odyssey* in classical Greek and medieval Latin do little more than offer ingenious fulfillments of Teiresias' prophecy of a death from the sea for Odysseus, leaving him spiritually marooned on Ithaca. It was Dante who first launched the hero forth from his home island—or rather from Circe's island before he ever returned home—on a spiritual quest. In the twenty-sixth canto of *Inferno* Dante comes with his guide Virgil to the eighth bolgia of Circle Eight, where the evil counselors move about endlessly, each concealed in a great horn of flame. There, enveloped in a double tongue of flame with his Iliadic comrade Diomedes, is Ulysses (the Romans' name for Odysseus), atoning, as Virgil explains, for his career as an arch-deceiver. So far Dante is following a post-Homeric, largely Latin, anti-Ulyssean tradition in which Ulysses is little more than a crafty, even criminal, trickster, the execrable strategist who engineered the theft of the Palladium, devised the Wooden Horse, and so destroyed Troy, Rome's spiritual mother-city. But then the tongue of flame quivers, and Ulysses is made to tell his own story. It is a story of the hero's relentless search for new experience. This is from John Ciardi's still unsurpassed translation of the *Commedia*:

> When I left Circe... who more than a year
> detained me near Gaeta long before
>
> Aeneas came and gave the place that name,
> not fondness for my son, nor reverence
> for my aged father, nor Penelope's claim
>
> to the joys of love, could drive out of my mind
> the lust to experience the far-flung world
> and the failings and felicities of mankind.
>
> I put out on the high and open sea
> with a single ship and only those few souls
> who stayed true when the rest deserted me.
>
> As far as Morocco and as far as Spain
> I saw both shores; and I saw Sardinia
> and the other islands of the open main.
>
> I and my men were stiff and slow with age
> when we sailed at last into the narrow pass
> where, warning all men back from further voyage,
>
> Hercules Pillars rose upon our sight.
> Already I had left Ceuta on the left;
> Seville now sank beside me on the right.
>
> "Shipmates," I said, "who through a hundred thousand
> perils have reached the West, do not deny
> to the brief remaining watch our senses stand

> experience of the world beyond the sun.
> Greeks! You were not born to live like brutes,
> but to press on toward manhood and recognition!"
>
> With this brief exhortation I made my crew
> so eager for the voyage I could hardly
> have held them back from it when I was through;
>
> and turning our stern toward morning, our bow toward night,
> we bore southwest out of the world of man;
> we made wings of our oars for our fool's flight.
>
> That night we raised the other pole ahead
> with all its stars, and ours had so declined
> it did not rise out of its ocean bed.
>
> Five times since we had dipped our bending oars
> beyond the world, the light beneath the moon
> had waxed and waned, when dead upon our course
>
> we sighted, dark in space, a peak so tall
> I doubted any man had seen the like.
> Our cheers were hardly sounded, when a squall
>
> broke hard upon our bow from the new land:
> three times it sucked the ship and the sea about
> as it pleased Another to order and command.
>
> At the fourth the poop rose and bow went down
> till the sea closed over us and the light was gone.[3]

This voyage into the Atlantic may have been suggested to Dante by accounts of the Celtic voyages of St. Brendan, but as an ending to Ulysses' adventures it is original with Dante. The moral allegory is clear enough: Ulysses is condemned as much for his inordinate desire for knowledge as for his deception; but it is also clear that Dante admires and identifies with the doomed hero's restless intellect and his passion to extend the horizon of human experience. It is the Renaissance Dante more than the medieval who engenders this new Ulysses, and he makes his next significant appearance in Tennyson's seventy-line lyric monologue, a poem too well known to require extensive quotation here. Tennyson blends into the hero's temper a measure of Byronic restlessness and contempt for domestic life and seasons it with a dash of Romantic wistfulness. His Ulysses broods and postures, but since in fact he never actually gets underway we never learn the outcome of his last voyage. It may be that the gulfs do wash him down, or it may be that he touches the Happy Isles and sees the great Achilles—we don't know. But we are convinced of his Victorian resolve

> To follow knowledge like a sinking star
> Beyond the utmost bounds of human thought,

and

> To strive, to seek, to find, and not to yield.[4]

Sixty years later, in 1904, the Italian poet Giovanni Pascoli published in his *Poemi conviviali* a narrative poem in twenty-four brief cantos (totaling 1200 lines) entitled *Ultimo Viaggio*. Pascoli has Odysseus in his last days seek, find nothing, and finally yield, but he does cast over the hero a beguiling *fin de siècle* enchantment. In the poem's opening cantos, Odysseus performs the inland pilgrimage prescribed by Teiresias and then returns home to sit by the fireside and wait for the prophesied death from the sea, *morte soave, molto soave*. But death delays nine years, and the old hero gradually sinks intro desolate reveries. He begins to doubt the reality of the experiences he had on his journey back from Troy to Ithaca. Penelope, shrewd and wise, understands what is happening to her aged husband, rouses him, and in the tenth spring Odysseus meets his old companions on the shore and sails forth with them on waves of nostalgia for the distant lands he visited on his perilous voyages. His earlier doubts are confirmed. Circe's island is deserted; the Cyclops never existed. Scylla and Charybdis are harmless landmarks, the Sirens are silent, and so forth. But on the rocks near the Sirens he sees the bones and shriveled skins of dead men and is musing silently on the symbolism when his ship cracks up on the reef. And the blue sea that loved Odysseus carries him on to the island of Calypso, and the concealing goddess finds his body on the shore and wraps her old, reluctant lover in the cloud of her hair and wails to the sterile sea, "Better not to be born, not to be at all is a smaller death than to be no more." These are the poem's closing lines, expressive of an existentialist preference for total non-being rather than a futile search for experience and the loss of awareness at death.[5] The best ending for a veteran hero and the true meaning of his experience is annihilation and absorption into the infinite. And this where we would leave Odysseus were it not for Nikos Kazantzakis.

Kazantzakis published his *Odyssey* in 1938. At 33,333 lines of demotic Greek iambic octometer, Kazantzakis' sequel is nearly three times the length of the Homeric original. Most critics agree that the length is fully justified by the rich development of the theme's content and symbolism. The poem is available in a splendid English translation by Kimon Friar.[6] I will attempt a three minute, thirty three second summary.

After a prologue to the sun, symbol of the ultimate purified spirit, the narrative begins with Odysseus, having just slain his wife's suitors, relaxing in his bath and reflecting on how bored he is already with the whole domestic scene. He puts his son Telemachus in charge of the island, gathers a motley crew, informs them that they are embarking to transform flesh into spirit, and sets sail for Sparta to see if he can interest Menelaus in further adventures. Menelaus has turned fat and lazy, but Helen is ready for action and sails off with Odysseus to Crete. His old crony Idomeneus is king of Knossos, but when he tries to make Helen his bride in the orgiastic bull rituals, Odysseus in disgust successfully leads a slave revolt against Idomeneus and marries Helen off to a young blond Dorian, a mingling of bloods that will engender the Greeks of the Golden Age. Then he sails off to Egypt in search of more adventures and the source of the Nile. In Egypt he unseals the tomb of an ancient pharaoh and appropriates the treasure, but when he finds himself thinking of settling down and building villas and estates on the Nile, he orders all the treasure dumped overboard. He then joins a young communist leader, a Jewish woman named Rala, in an unsuccessful revolt against the pharaoh, is thrown into prison, is released when he frightens the pharaoh with a mask he carved of the tormented face of a new god, gathers together a following of persecuted outcasts and leads them out of Egypt. They discover the source of the Nile at the foot of a mountain. Odysseus sets his people to building what he hopes will be a utopian city and himself ascends the mountain, communes with his god there for seven days, and then descends, bringing his people new commandments by which to live: 1) cultivate the mind and so impose order on disorder; 2) transcend the mind with the heart and so pierce to the essence of being; 3) become free of the hope that both mind and heart offer; and 4) plumb the atavistic roots of ego, race, and species and enter into a mystic communion with the entire universe. God is a struggling evolutionary growth of the spirit through all phenomena. The city is built in the Land of the Heart's Desire, and on the first day of its inaugural rites, the mountain erupts in a volcanic explosion and destroys the city utterly. All his companions are lost. Odysseus plunges into a timeless contemplation blazing with light and becomes one with all animate and inanimate beings. Fireflies glow in his beard; his feet flow like rivers. He has become a great ascetic now, with the thirty-two marks of the perfect man, abandoning the cult of doing for the cultivation of being. But his travels continue. He begins a long, southward trek through the heart of the dark continent, encountering along the way a succession of various seekers, a Siddhartha, a mystic courtesan, a poet, a Don Quixote, and Epicurean, a sacrificial king, and finally, at the southernmost tip of Africa, a young black Christ-like fisherman. Then the great ascetic builds a coffin-like kayak and embarks on his last journey, sailing past the clashing rocks of Yes and No toward the South Pole. Death, his old and faithful friend, comes and sits on the prow, turning into a Black Swan, into Dante's White Rose, into an iceberg, Odysseus' last ship of Death. The cold South Wind strips him bare, he summons all those whose spirits his own spirit has ever joined, and they all hear the cry of the World Destroyer—Helen also, herself dying, nursed by her granddaughters on the banks of the Eurotas River near Sparta, and rising up when she hears Odysseus' cry and saying, "Dear God, if only I could wreck my family once more and feel the wind in my face as I stand on the prow"— and then Odysseus' flesh dissolves and the great mind leaps to the peak of its holy freedom. The poem ends with an epilogue to the setting Sun, come home at last, signaling the completion of the transmutation of matter into spirit and light.

Let us now complete the process of turning Homer's *Odyssey* inside out. From the very beginning of Homer's *Odyssey*, Odysseus is preeminently the hero who operates on the level of *noos*, mind. In Homer that mind, with all its cunning and depth, is bent on achieving *nostos*, a return home. In a tradition that begins really with Dante, knowledge and experience become the goal of a quest that leads the hero away from home—or towards his true home, when we recall the original meaning of both *noos* and *nostos*. The identity of the words was established in 1978 by Douglas Frame, who derived *noos* and *nostos* from an Indo-European root *NES, meaning to return from darkness to light. Frame sees the psycholinguistic identity of *noos* and *nostos* preserved structurally in Homer's poem, reviving the old idea of Odysseus as a solar hero who comes to light after a period of darkness. This can be seen as the operative archetype in the sequel tradition as well, especially as consummated by Kazantzakis, whose poem is framed and shot through with images of light, and who has his hero exclaim, "O my soul, your voyages have been your native land." The post-Homeric impulse to have Odysseus sail off on one more voyage is more than just nostalgia to see the old pro in action once more. Odysseus' homecoming is not complete until his enlightenment is complete. Neoplatonic philosophers allegorized Homer's *Odyssey* along similar lines, seeing Odysseus as a type of rational man passing through the sublunary universe, acquiring gnosis, and returning to his celestial home.

This long story of Odysseus striving toward and finally achieving cosmic enlightenment ultimately flows from the open quality of Homer's mind, with Odysseus as a kind of emanation from Homer's mind through poetic time. The whole sequel tradition, and Kazantzakis especially, can be seen as a series of responses, or one cumulative response, to a *kong-an* Homer poses in the *Odyssey*: Odysseus' mind, *noos*, and his homecoming, *nostos*, are they the same or different? But that response, culminating in the grand, mystical merging with the world soul in Kazantzakis' sequel, would be judged by any Zen master as fifty per-cent—only halfway there, stuck in the realm of the absolute and lacking the compassionate, functional engagement with the situation and people at hand that characterizes complete enlightenment. And, like many Zen masters, Homer answers his own question, dramatizing his answer in the climactic scene of the *Odyssey*, the scene in which Odysseus and Penelope lock eyebrows after twenty years of separation. Here finally Odysseus is stripped of the cunning that enabled him to survive but kept him separate; and Penelope, seeing her husband's total exposure, is able to drop her self-protective caution.

The scene in Odysseus' palace is illuminated by firelight. Odysseus has just slain the band of arrogant and violent young men who had been courting his wife, trying to kill his son, and eating him out of house and home. He is still in the guise of an old beggar, covered with blood from the battle, when Penelope comes down from her quarters to see the man who has killed her suitors.

> Penelope descended the stairs, her heart
> In turmoil. Should she hold back and question   XXIII.90
> Her husband? Or should she go up to him,
> Embrace him, and kiss his hands and head?
> She entered the hall, crossing the stone threshold,
> And sat opposite Odysseus, in the firelight
> Beside the farther wall. He sat by a column,
> Looking down, waiting to see if his incomparable wife
> Would say anything to him when she saw him.
> She sat a long time in silence, wondering.
> She would look at his face and see her husband,
> But then fail to know him in his dirty rags.   100
> Telemachus couldn't take it any more:

> "Mother, how can you be so hard,
> Holding back like that? Why don't you sit
> Next to father and talk to him, ask him things?
> No other woman would have the heart
> To stand off from her husband who has come back
> After twenty hard years to his country and home.
> But your heart is always colder than stone."

And Penelope, cautious as ever:

> "My child, I am lost in wonder
> And unable to speak or ask a question
> Or look him in the eyes. If he really is
> Odysseus come home, the two of us
> Will be sure of each other, very sure.
> There are secrets between us no one else knows."

Odysseus, who had borne much, smiled,
And his words flew to his son on wings:

> "Telemachus, let your mother test me
> In our hall. She will soon see more clearly.
> Now, because I am dirty and wearing rags,   100
> She is not ready to acknowledge who I am."

...
Odysseus, meanwhile, was being bathed
By the housekeeper, Eurynome. She
Rubbed him with olive oil and threw about him
A beautiful cloak and tunic. And Athena
Shed beauty upon him, and made him look
Taller and more muscled, and made his hair
Tumble down his head like hyacinth flowers.

Imagine a craftsman overlaying silver
With pure gold. He has learned his art
From Pallas Athena and Lord Hephaestus,
And creates works of breathtaking beauty.

So Athena herself made his head and shoulders
Shimmer with grace. He came from the bath
Like a god, and sat down on the chair again
Opposite his wife, and spoke to her and said:

"You're a mysterious woman.
            The gods
Have given to you, more than to any
Other woman, an unyielding heart.
No other woman would be able to endure
Standing off from her husband, come back
After twenty hard years to his country and home.
Nurse, make up a bed for me so I can lie down
Alone, since her heart is a cold lump of iron."

And Penelope, cautious and wary:
"You're a mysterious man.
 I am not being proud
Or scornful, nor am I bewildered—not at all.
I know very well what you looked like
When you left Ithaca on your long-oared ship.
Nurse, bring the bed out from the master bedroom,
The bedstead he made himself, and spread it for him
With fleeces and blankets and silky coverlets."

She was testing her husband.
And Odysseus
Could bear no more, and cried out to his wife:

"By God, woman, now you've cut deep.
Who moved my bed? It would be hard
For anyone, no matter how skilled, to move it.
A god could come down and move it easily,
But not a man alive, however young and strong,
Could ever pry it up. There's something telling
About how that bed's built, and no one else
Built it but me.

          There was an olive tree
Growing on the site, long-leaved and full,
Its trunk thick as a post. I built my bedroom
Around that tree, and when I had finished
The masonry walls and done the roofing   200
And set in the jointed, close-fitting doors,
I lopped off all of the olive's branches,
Trimmed the trunk from the root on up,
And rounded it and trued it with an adze until
I had myself a bedpost. I bored it with an auger,
And starting from this I framed up the whole bed,
Inlaying it with gold and silver and ivory
And stretching across it oxhide thongs dyed purple.
So there's our secret. But I do not know, woman,
Whether my bed is still firmly in place, or if   210
Some other man has cut through the olive's trunk."

At this, Penelope finally let go.
Odysseus had shown he knew their old secret.
In tears, she ran straight to him, threw her arms
Around him, kissed his face, and said:

"Don't be angry with me, Odysseus. You,
Of all men, know how the world goes.
It is the gods who gave us sorrow, the gods
Who begrudged us a life together, enjoying
Our youth and arriving side by side   220
To the threshold of old age. Don't hold it against me
That when I first saw you I didn't welcome you
As I do now. My heart has been cold with fear
That an imposter would come and deceive me.
There are many who scheme for ill-gotten gains.
Not even Helen, daughter of Zeus,
Would have slept with a foreigner had she known
The Greeks would go to war to bring her back home.
It was a god who drove her to that dreadful act,
Or she never would have thought of doing what she did,   230
The horror that brought suffering to us as well.
But now, since you have confirmed the secret
Of our marriage bed, which no one has ever seen—
Only you and I and a single servant, Actor's daughter,
Whom my father gave me before I ever came here
And who kept the doors of our bridal chamber—
You have persuaded even my stubborn heart."

This brought tears from deep within him,
And as he wept he clung to his beloved wife.

> Land is a welcome sight to men swimming 240
> For their lives, after Poseidon has smashed their ship
> In heavy seas. Only a few of them escape
> And make it to shore. They come out
> Of the grey water crusted with brine, glad
> To be alive and set foot on dry land.

> So welcome a sight was her husband to her.
> She would not loosen her white arms from his neck,
> And rose-fingered Dawn would have risen
> On their weeping, had not Athena stepped in
> And held back the long night at the end of its course 250
> And stopped gold-stitched Dawn at Ocean's shores
> From yoking the horses that bring light to men,
> Lampus and Phaethon, the colts of Dawn.

Odysseus' homecoming is almost complete. Two minds have become one, but one more step is necessary, and Athena delays the light, the final dawn of the *Odyssey*, until the correct function of Odysseus' and Penelope intimacy can be enacted. Penelope and Odysseus talk.

> While they spoke to one another,
> Eurynome and the nurse made the bed
> By torchlight, spreading it with soft coverlets.
> Then the old nurse went to her room to lie down,
> And Eurynome, who kept the bedroom,
> Led the couple to their bed, lighting the way. 300
> When she had led them in, she withdrew,
> And they went with joy to their bed
> And to their rituals of old.

The full presentation of a *kong-an* consists of a story, one or more questions, and a brief commentary in prose or verse. You have just heard the story. Here are the questions:

> 1. Odysseus' mind and Penelope's mind, which one do you like?
>
> 2. Homer's mind and your mind, are they the same or different?

And the poem:

> Eye like a shooting star,
> Mind like lightning's
> You for the first time will know you are home,
> When you welcome the stranger at your door.

Stanley Lombardo
University of Kansas

Notes

1. See Robert Aitken, *The Gateless Barrier—The Wu-Men Kuan*, (San Francisco: North Point Press, 1990).
2. Jacques Lusseyran, *And There Was Light*, second edition (New York: Parabola Books, 1998), pp 16–17.
3. Dante Alighieri, *The Divine Comedy*, trans. John Ciardi (New York: Norton, 1977).
4. Alfred, Lord Tennyson, "Ulysses," in *Poetry of the Victorian Period*, third edition, ed. Jerome Buckley and George Woods (Glenview, Illinois: Scott, Foresman and Company, 1965), 43–44.
5. Giovanni Pascoli, *Poemi conviviali* (Milano: A. Mondadori, 1980).
6. Kazantzakis, Nicos, *The Odyssey; a modern sequel*, trans. Kimon Friar (New York: Simon and Schuster, 1958).

Recent Translations of the Odyssey

Homer. *The Odyssey*. Trans. Robert Fagles. New York: Viking, 1996.

Homer. *The Odyssey*. Trans. Robert Fitzgerald. Garden City, New York: Doubleday, 1961.

Homer. *The Odyssey of Homer*. Trans. Richmond Lattimore. New York: Harper and Row, 1965.

Homer. *The Odyssey*. Trans. Stanley Lombardo. Indianapolis and Cambridge: Hackett, 2000.

Homer. *The Odyssey of Homer*. Trans. Allen Mandelbaum. Berkeley: University of California Press, 1990.

Homer. *The Odyssey*. Trans. Walter Shewring. Oxford: Oxford University Press, 1980.

Suggestions for Further Reading

Ahl, Frederick, and Roisman, Hanna M. *The Odyssey Re-Formed.* Ithaca: Cornell University Press, 1996.

Allen, T. W., ed. *Homeri Opera.* 2nd ed. vols. III and IV. Oxford Classical Texts. London and New York: Oxford University Press, 1917.

Arnold, Matthew. "On Translating Homer." In *On the Classical Tradition.* Ed. by R. H. Super. Ann Arbor and London: Michigan University Press, 1960.

Auerbach, Erich. *Mimesis: The Representation of Reality in Western Literature.* Trans. by Willard Trask. Chapter 1, "Odysseus' Scar." Princeton: Princeton University Press, 1953.

Austin, Norman. *Archery at the Dark of the Moon: Poetic Problems in Homer's* Odyssey. Berkeley: University of California Press, 1975.

Beye, Charles R. *The Iliad, the Odyssey, and the Epic Tradition.* New York and London: Anchor Books, 1966.

Bloom, Harold, ed. *Homer's Odyssey.* New York: Chelsea Books, 1988.

Buitron, Diana, and Cohen, Beth, eds. *The Odyssey and Ancient Art: An Epic in Word and Image.* Annandale-on-Hudson, New York: The Edith C. Blum Art Institute, Bard College, 1992.

Carter, Jane B., and Morris, Sarah P., eds. *The Ages of Homer: A Tribute to Emily Townsend Vermeule.* Austin: University of Texas Press, 1995.

Clarke, Howard. *The Art of the Odyssey.* Englewood Cliffs, N.J.: Prentice-Hall., 1967.

—. *Homer's Readers: A Historical Introduction to the Iliad and the Odyssey.* Newark, Del.: University of Delaware Press, 1981.

Clay, Jenny Strauss. *The Wrath of Athena: Gods and Men in the Odyssey.* Princeton: Princeton University Press, 1983.

Cohen, Beth, ed. *The Distaff Side: Representing the Female in Homer's Odyssey.* New York and London: Oxford University Press, 1995.

A Commentary on Homer's Odyssey. Vol. 1: books I–VIII, A. Heubeek, S. West, J. B. Hainsworth. Vol. II: books IX–XVI, A. Heubeck, A. Hoekstra. Vol. III: books XVII–XXIV, J. Russo, M. Fernández-Galiano, A. Heubeck. New York and Oxford: Oxford University Press, 1988–92.

Cook, Erwin R. *The Odyssey in Athens: Myths of Cultural Origins.* Ithaca, N.Y.: Cornell University Press, 1995.

Dawe, R. D. *The Odyssey: Translation and Analysis.* Lewes: Book Guild, *1993.*

Doherty, Lilhan Eileen. *Siren Songs: Gender, Audiences, and Narrators in the* Odyssey. Ann Arbor: University of Michigan Press, 1995.

Felson, Nancy. *Regarding Penelope: From Character to Poetics.* rev. paperback ed. Norman: University of Oklahoma Press, 1997.

Finley, M. I. *The World of Odysseus.* 2nd rev. ed. Harmondsworth: Penguin, 1979.

Frame, Douglas. *The Myth of Return in Early Greek Epic.* New Haven: Yale University Press, 1978.

Griffin, Jasper. *Homer on Life and Death.* Oxford: Clarendon Press, 1980.

Homer. *The Odyssey.* Ed. with English translation by A. T. Murray, revised by George E. Dimock. 2 vols. The Loeb Classical Library. Cambridge, Mass., and London: Harvard University Press, 1995.

Katz, Marilyn A. *Penelope's Renown: Meaning and Indeterminacy in the Odyssey.* Princeton: Princeton University Press, 1991.

Kirk, G. S. *The Songs of Homer.* Cambridge, England: Cambridge University Press, 1962.

Lamberton, R., and Keaney, J. J., eds. *Homer's Ancient Readers: The Hermeneutics of Greek Epic's Earliest Exegetes.* Princeton: Princeton University Press, 1992.

Lord, Albert. *The Singer of Tales.* Cambridge, Mass.: Harvard University Press, 1960.

——. *The Singer Resumes the Tale.* Ed. by M. L. Lord. Ithaca, N.Y.: Cornell University Press, 1995.

Morris, Ian, and Powell, Barry, eds. *A New Companion to Homer.* Leiden, Netherlands: Brill., 1997.

Moulton, Carroll. *Similes in the Homeric Poems.* Göttingen, Germany: Vandenhoeck und Ruprecht., 1977.

Murnaghan, Sheila. *Disguise and Recognition in the Odyssey.* Princeton: Princeton University Press, 1987.

Myrsiades, Kostas, ed. *Approaches to Teaching Homer's Iliad and Odyssey.* New York: Modern Language Association, 1987.

Nagy, Gregory. *The Best of Achaeans: Concepts of the Hero in Archaic Greek Poetry.* rev. ed. Baltimore and London: Johns Hopkins University Press, 1999.

Page, Denys. *Folktales in Homer's Odyssey.* Cambridge, Mass.: Harvard University Press, 1973.

——. *The Homeric Odyssey.* Oxford: Clarendon Press, 1955.

Parry, Milman. *The Making of Homeric Verse: The Collected Papers of Milman Parry.* Ed. by Adam Parry. Oxford: Clarendon Press, 1971.

Peradotto, John. *Man in the Middle Voice: Name and Narration in the Odyssey.* Martin Classical Lectures, New Series, vol. I. Princeton: Princeton University Press, 1990.

Puccii, Pietro. *Odysseus Polutropos: Intertextual Readings in the Odyssey and the Iliad.* 2nd ed. Ithaca, New York: Cornell University Press, 1995.

Reece, Steve. *The Stranger's Welcome: The Aesthetics of the Homeric Hospitality Scene.* Ann Arbor: University of Michigan Press, 1993.

Rubens, Beaty, and Taplin, Oliver. *An Odyssey Round Odysseus: The Man and His Story Traced Through Time and Place.* London: BBC Books, 1989.

Rutherford, R. B. *Homer.* Greece and Rome. New surveys in the classics, no. 26. Oxford: Oxford University Press, 1994.

Schein, Seth, ed. *Reading the Odyssey: Selected Interpretive Essays.* Princeton: Princeton University Press, 1996.

Scully, Stephen. *Homer and the Sacred City.* Ithaca and London: Cornell University Press, 1990.

Segal, Charles. *Singers, Heroes, and Gods in the Odyssey.* Ithaca and London: Cornell University Press, 1994.

Stanford, W. B., ed. *The Odyssey.* 2nd ed. 2 vols. London and New York: Macmillan, 1967.

—. *The Ulysses Theme: A Study in the Adaptability of the Homeric Hero.* Oxford: Oxford University Press, 1983.

Steiner, George, and Fagles, Robert, eds. *Homer: A Collection of Critical Essays.* Ed. by Maynard Mack. Twentieth Century Views. Englewood Cliffs, N.J.: Prentice-Hall, 1962.

Thalmann, William G. *The Odyssey: Poem of Return.* New York: Twayne, 1992.

—. *The Swineherd and the Bow: Representations of Class in the Odyssey.* Ithaca: Cornell University Press, 1998.

Tracy, Stephen W. *The Story of the Odyssey.* Princeton: Princeton University Press, 1990.

Vivante, Paolo. *Homer.* New Haven and London: Yale University Press, 1985.

—. *Homeric Rhythm: A Philosophical Study.* Westport, Conn.: Greenwood Press, 1997.

Wace, Alan J. B., and Stubbings, Frank. *A Companion to Homer.* London: Macmillan, 1962.

Whitman, Cedric H. *Homer and the Heroic Tradition.* Cambridge, Mass., and London: Harvard University Press, 1958.

Discussion Questions

Why does Odysseus seemingly place "homecoming" above every other aspiration?

How powerful or autonomous is Athena in her support of Odysseus? Is she more than the daughter/agent of Zeus?

The Odyssey is a series of tales within tales—bards, storytellers, heroes and heroines all retell events. What is the role of fact and fiction, truth and deception, in these retellings?

Calypso's name means "the burier" and "the concealer," and yet what she offers Odysseus is immortality. What sense does this make?

One minute Odysseus contemplates suicide and not long afterwards clings desperately to life. What changed his mind?

Is there any significance to the fact that Odysseus' last words to Nausicaa are the same as Telemachus' last words to Helen?

What is the importance of Odysseus' journey to the netherworld? Is it significant that this episode lies at the center of the poem?

Circe is able to give Odysseus nearly the same information as Tiresias; so why is it important for Odysseus to encounter Tiresias?

Is Odysseus at first impressed or disappointed with his son Telemachus? Why?

How necessary and justified is the final slaughter of the suitors, *all* of them, as well as the compromised servant women? Is it only rage and revenge that drives Odysseus in the end? Does he confirm or diminish his status as hero in these acts?

How do Odysseus and Penelope reveal themselves to each other not only in their true identities but also in their perfect suitability to each other?

Discussion Points

• The narrative structure of the *Odyssey*, the flashbacks and use of parallel time-sequences.

• The significance of Telemachus' journey into and encounter with the world of his father in the courts of Nestor and Menelaus.

• Odysseus as master-liar, i.e., the role that his deceptions play in his homecoming.

• Odysseus as a returning warrior suffering from PTSD (Post-traumatic Stress Disorder).

• The role of time and of time's passing in the *Odyssey*. For years Penelope weaves and unweaves her tapestry. For years too, Odysseus revisits the same waters and watches the waves come in and go out.

• Odysseus' identification with the victim-woman in the Phaeacian bard's account of the rape of the royal house of Priam.

• The central role of "secret signs" and of recognition scenes in the *Odyssey*.

• The role of "donor figures" in the story and in Odysseus' survival.

• The relationship between Odysseus and his father, past and present.

• The role of fabric and garments in the poem, particularly as the domain of women, human and divine. Penelope's tapestry and Ino's cloak as protective garments.

• The relationship between Odysseus and Poseidon. The god is the source of most of the hero's woes, and yet Odysseus becomes his missionary, whose sweet death will come from the sea.

Points for Further Investigation

• The *Odyssey* as the *Iliad*'s sequel, complement, and completion.

• The narrative and aesthetic role played by Homer's extended similes (italicized in the Lombardo translation).

• The Sirens as a fascination and focus for later poetry and art.

• The uncontrolled savagery of Odysseus in the *Odyssey* and of Achilles in the *Iliad* as reflective of ancient warfare and its consummate warriors.

RAMAYANA

We turn next to the oldest extant version of a story that in one form or another has beguiled and mesmerized the Hindu populations of South Asia for over 2000 years—the classical Indian work known as the *Ramayana* ("The Exploits of Rama"). Traditionally ascribed to the poet-sage Valmiki, the Sanskrit text contains seven books recounting the life and adventures of the lordly King Rama, later believed to be an incarnation of the great god Vishnu. Often construed by Westerners alongside the *Mahabharata* as one of the two great epic poems of ancient India, the Valmiki *Ramayana* is designated in the Sanskrit tradition as the first or foundational poem (*adikavya*) of Indian classical literature, but like the longer epic, it derived from a well developed tradition of oral composition and transmission. As Wendy Doniger points out in the introduction to her fascinating essay, the story retold here of jealousy and intrigue in the court of King Dasharatha, of Prince Rama's selfless voluntary exile to the forest with his devoted wife Sita and loyal brother Lakshmana, of Sita's forcible abduction by Ravana the treacherous king of the rakshasas and the climactic battle between Ravana's demonic forces and Rama's monkey allies which later ensues, and finally, the long-delayed return of Sita and her shocking repudiation by Rama at the end—all of this has constituted the stuff of living legend for millions of South Asians over the past two millennia or more. With its kaleidoscopic vision of reality, its miraculous adventures and high-minded monkey business, and its anguished story of treachery, loyalty, and love, this story makes a spell-binding contribution to world literature.

Ramayana Timeline

2400–1700	Indus Valley Civilization
1500	Aryan migrations
1200	Compilation of Hymns of the Rig Veda
900–700	Brahmanas
700–300	Classical Upanishads
563–483	Siddhartha Gautama, the Buddha
500 [–200C.E.]	Development of the *Mahabharata*
200 [–200C.E.]	*Bhagavad Gita*
400 [–200C.E.]	Development of the *Ramayana*
350	Panini, grammarian of classical Sanskrit
326	Alexander the Great invades western India
269–232	Reign of Ashoka, first Buddhist king
B.C.E.	
C.E.	
12c	Kamban's Tamil Ramayana, *Iramavataram*
1532–1623	Tulsidas, author of *Ramcaritmanas*, the Hindi Ramayana

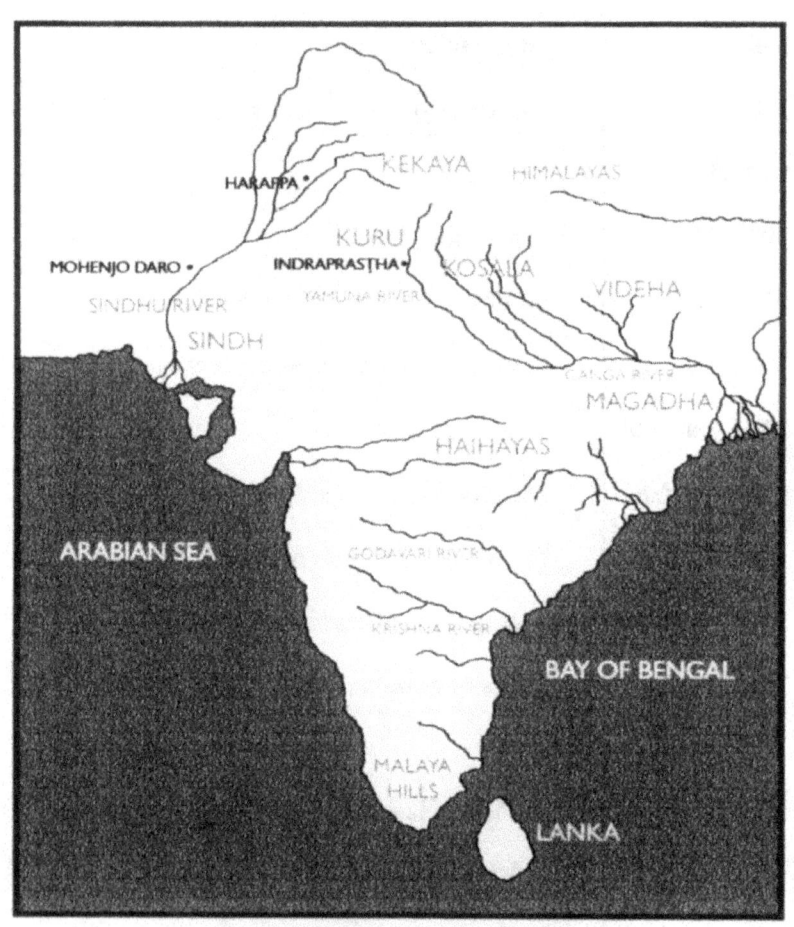

ANCIENT INDIA

SHADOWS OF THE RAMAYANA

Introduction

The *Ramayana*, composed by the sage Valmiki in Sanskrit in Northern India some time between the second century BCE and the second century CE, is the oldest surviving text of a story that has continued to be retold for over two thousand years, in Sanskrit dramas and poetry, in Hindi and Bengali and Tamil retellings, in *Amar Chitra Katha* comic books (India's version of Classic Comics), on film, on television, on political posters.[1] The earliest recorded version, in the Sanskrit text of Valmiki, establishes this plot of the central episode that I will focus on in this essay:

> Sita, the wife of Prince Rama, had been born from a furrow of the earth. The demon king Ravana stole Sita from Rama and kept her captive on the island of Lanka for many years. Rama enlisted the help of an army of monkeys and finally killed Ravana and brought Sita back home with him. But then he said he feared that his people worried that Sita's reputation, if not her chastity, had been sullied by her long sojourn in the house of another man. He forced Sita to undergo an ordeal by fire: she swore that she had always been faithful to Rama, called on the fire to protect her, and entered the blazing flame; but the god of Fire placed her in Rama's lap, assuring him that Sita had always been pure in thought as well as deed. Rama reinstated her, but when he doubted her again she disappeared forever back into the earth.[2]

The central human characters of the Valmiki *Ramayana*—Rama the perfect prince, Sita his perfect wife, and Lakshmana his perfect brother (later to form the template for the perfect worshipper of the now deified Rama)—were born to be paradigms, squeaky clean, goody-goodies (or, in the case of the perfectly demonic demon Ravana, a baddy-baddy). If that were all there was to the *Ramayana*, it would have proved ideologically useful to people interested in enforcing moral standards or in rallying religious fanatics—as it has proved all too capable of doing—but it would probably not have survived as a beloved work of great literature, as it has also done. Rama is an incarnate god in the original Sanskrit text, though often he seems to forget that he is, and has to be reminded of it, and more often it does not seem to be an issue at all. But even in Sanskrit, god is in the details, and the details of the *Ramayana* are what give it its character. More precisely, each of the major human characters has at least two doubles, a double among the monkeys who help Rama kill Ravana and retrieve Sita, and a double among the demons in the family of Ravana. All the fun is in the monkeys and demons. The humans, and indeed the demons, also have a number of temporary doubles, illusions created at particular moments in the Epic to fool someone. And, finally, in the later retellings of the *Ramayana*, the ones that came after Valmiki's Sanskrit text, the doubles proliferate to an even greater extent. These illusory characters are, ironically, more flesh and blood, as we would say, more complex and nuanced than the human characters that they mirror; or, rather, added to those original characters they provide the nuances of ambiguity and ambivalence that constitute the depth and substance of the total character, composed of the original plus the shadow. In addition, a number of myths are introduced as narrative shadows of the central plot, a few inserted in the main story, but most of them added in books 1 and 7. These myths supply a constant commentary on the central story, within the text, developing over the centuries.

Human Shadows

Let us begin with characters who serve as doubles of other characters within the *Ramayana*, and let us start with the human doubles, and among them, the females. There are a lot of females. The childless king Dasharatha obtains a magic porridge, infused with the essence of Vishnu, to share among his queens; he gives half to Kausalya, who bears him Rama; 3/8 to Sumitra, who bears him the twins Lakshmana and Shatrughna (each made of 3/16 of Vishnu), and 1/8 to Kaikeyi, who bears him Bharata. When it is time for Rama, the eldest, to ascend the throne, Kaikeyi uses sexual blackmail (among other things) to force Dasharatha to put her son, Bharata, on the throne instead, and send Rama into exile, where Ravana steals Sita and the plot, as they say, thickens. Kaikeyi is the evil shadow of the good queen, Kausalya. But Kaikeyi herself is absolved of her evil by having it displaced onto the old hunchback Manthara, who corrupts Kaikeyi and forces her, against Kaikeyi's better judgement, to act as she does. Shatrughna puns on Manthara's name, saying that it was she who churned up (*manth*) for them the ocean of grief, in which Kaikeyi was the sea-serpent (*graha*),[3] and much later, when Sita sees Ravana coming to kill her, she curses Manthara and blames her sinister counsels for bringing about the sufferings that will overwhelm Kausalya, the mother of Rama. On the other hand, when Shatrughna drags Manthara around, he yells curses on Kaikeyi. In this text, even the shadows have shadows.

Turning now to the male human doubles, we have seen that all four brothers are fragments of a single person, incarnations of Vishnu. Lakshmana functions as the shadow of Rama: Rama is called "Saha-Lakshmana" ("With-Lakshmana") as if the accompaniment of his brother were a constant quality, like the color of his eyes, and Lakshmana is the one who speaks out what Rama is too much of a boyscout to say.[4] After Dasharatha has disinherited and banished Rama, and Rama has quietly acquiesced, other people, but never Rama, complain loudly: first, briefly, Rama's mother, and then Lakshmana, who says, "I don't like this. The king is perverse, old, and debauched by pleasures. What would he not say under pressure, mad with passion as he is? Rama hasn't done anything wrong. What son would take to heart the words of a king who has become a child again? Before anyone learns of this, let me help you seize control of the government. I will slaughter everyone who takes Bharata's side. Now that the king has made me and you his enemies, who will help him make Bharata the king?" But Rama replies, "It is not within my power to defy my father's bidding. I bow my head in supplication; I wish to go to the forest. I appreciate your love and loyalty, but you don't understand the meaning of life; give up your violence and be righteous like me." Lakshmana can't bear it; he sighs and his eyes bulge, and he accuses Rama of panicking like a wimp; where Rama talks of fate, Lakshmana says he will demonstrate that the power of a man's action is greater than fate. Rama tells Bharata always to defer to Dasharatha, but Lakshmana replies, in fury, "I can no longer regard the great king as my father after the way he abandoned Rama."

On the other hand, the text suggests that Rama might fear that his brother Lakshmana might become another sort of double, that he could replace Rama in bed with Sita. A man's fear of being cuckolded by his younger brother is endemic to South Asian culture; the *niyoga* or Levirate that allows a widow to conceive a child by her dead husband's brother makes the lawmaker Manu very nervous,[5] and the *Kamasutra* warns that a woman who marries the oldest of several brothers is likely to commit adultery with them.[6] The Valmiki *Ramayana* keeps insisting that Lakshmana will *not* sleep with Sita; it doth protest too much. Lakshmana himself makes the delightfully ambiguous remark, "How could I find sleep, or indeed happiness, while Rama is lying with Sita on the ground."[7]

The tension between the two brothers, over Sita, is a major motivation for the plot. In the forest, Rama goes off to hunt a deer, and tells Lakshmana to guard Sita. Sita thinks she hears Rama calling (it is a trick, about which more below) and urges Lakshmana to find and help Rama. Lakshmana says Rama can take care of himself. Sita taunts Lakshmana, saying, "You are so perverse. You think that if Rama dies you can have me, but I will never let you possess me. Bharata has gotten you to follow Rama, as his spy. That's what it must be. And you've stayed here in order to get me, lusting after me while pretending to be a friend. And that's why you won't come to his aid. But I will never have anything to do with any man but Rama." Lakshmana gets angry and stalks off, leaving Sita totally unprotected; and Ravana comes and gets Sita. When Rama returns, he says to Lakshmana, "You should not have come here just because an angry woman teased you. Submitting to Sita and to your own anger has caused you to violate *dharma*." Indeed, why would Sita have said such a thing if she didn't believe it on some level? And why would it have made Lakshmana so mad if there weren't some truth in it? When Rama, hunting for Sita, finds the cloak and jewels that she dropped as Ravana abducted her, he says to Lakshmana, "Do you recognize any of this?" And Lakshmana replies, as if butter wouldn't melt in his mouth, "I have never looked at any part of Sita but her feet, so I recognize the anklets, but not the rest of her things."

Finally, after Sita has been restored and rejected (about which, too, more below), Rama is tricked into having to kill Lakshmana. This happens as the result of a rather elaborate (but not atypical, in this Epic) set of vows and curses. Death, incarnate, comes to talk with Rama and makes him promise to kill anyone who tries to interrupt them; Lakshmana guards the door. An ascetic arrives and threatens to destroy the world if Lakshmana won't let him see Rama; Lakshmana therefore interrupts Rama and Death, choosing the lesser of two evils: his own death. Rama then says that, for Lakshmana, being separated from him (Rama) would be so terrible that it would be the equivalent of death, and so he satisfies the curse by merely banishing Lakshmana—who then commits suicide. Does this episode represent a displaced, suppressed desire of Rama to kill Lakshmana? If so, it is thoroughly submerged, one might even say repressed, on the human plane, but it bursts out in the animal world.

Animals

Let us therefore now consider the animal doubles: male monkeys. In a word, the wrong monkeys function as the shadows of Bharata and Rama. There are a number of parallels between monkeys and people in general in the *Ramayana*, both explicit and implicit.[8] Although people assume that they cannot understand the language of the deer (as is remarked on the occasion when Rama goes off to hunt the deer that renders Sita vulnerable), they can understand the language of monkeys, the deer of the trees (as they are called in Sanskrit). Monkeys are like people, and are incarnate gods, as the great heroes are.[9] In the forest, after Sita has been stolen, Rama and Lakshmana meet Sugriva, who used to be king of the monkeys and claims that his brother Valin stole his wife and throne; Rama sides with Sugriva and murders Valin by shooting him in the back, an episode that has long troubled the South Asian tradition. Why does he do it? Apparently because Rama senses a parallel between his situation and that of Sugriva and therefore sides with Sugriva against his brother: each of them has lost his wife and has a brother occupying the throne that was to be his. But if Sugriva is Rama, who is Valin?

The answer to this question lies in the more specific parallels between the things that happen to the monkey brothers and the things that happen to the human brothers. For instance, when Sugriva first sees Rama and Lakshmana, he thinks Valin sent them, just as Lakshmana, seeing Bharata approach them in the forest, thinks he has come to fight them. Both of them are wrong, overreacting with a kind of paranoia. After Lakshmana has told Hanuman of Rama's troubles, Hanuman says to Rama, speaking of Sugriva, "He is exiled from his kingdom and is hated by his brother Valin, who has stolen his wife and left him abandoned in the forest." Now, this is not exactly true of Sugriva; the first point is pretty true (he is exiled), but the second is not (Valin doesn't hate Sugriva; Sugriva hates Valin), and the third is not exactly true either: Sugriva carried off Valin's consort first, and when Valin retaliated, Sugriva fled out of guilt and terror. Nor is any of this true of any single enemy of Rama (if we take Rama as a parallel to Sugriva); it was Dasharatha who exiled Rama and caused him to flee to the forest; there is no enmity between Rama and Bharata, though Bharata occupies Rama's throne; and it was Ravana who carried off Rama's consort. If Sugriva is Rama, then, Valin is a combination of Dasharatha, Ravana, and Bharata (as well as Lakshmana, who, as we have seen, has a problematic relationship with Sita). If we try to hang on to this as a parallel, it is a pretty messy parallel. In fact, Rama sides with the wrong monkey: Valin, like Rama, is the *older* brother, the true heir, the legal parallel to Rama, as Sugriva is not. Yet the main implication of Hanuman's speech is true: Rama sympathizes with Sugriva because both of them have lost their wives and both now have brothers on their thrones. The situations are the same, but the villains are entirely different—and this is what Rama fails to notice.

This is the sense in which the monkeys are the shadows of the human brothers, or rather, side-shadows, to use the term coined by Gary Saul Morson (after Bakhtin): they suggest what might have been.[10] The monkeys are not merely Valmiki's projections, nor projections from Rama's mind; they are, rather, literary fractions, symbolic layers, parallel lives. The monkey story is not merely accidentally appended; it is a telling variant of the life of Rama. But it does not mirror that life exactly; it is a mythological transformation, taking the pieces and rearranging them to make a slightly different pattern, as the dreamwork does, according to Freud. And just as the shadow Kaikeyi had her own shadow, the hunchback Manthara, so, here, even the metaphorical shadows, the monkeys, have real shadows. Hanuman's shadow is even detachable, like Peter Pan's: a demoness tries to steal it when he is flying across the water to Lanka, and he has to enter her to get it back again. In later tellings, that shadow of his impregnates her, though Hanuman himself, proud of his chastity, is unaware of this.[11] In the case of this unconscious sexual encounter, the shadow is more substantial than its prototype.

Demons

Let us now consider demon doubles, again beginning with the males. Demons, in general, are explicitly said to be projected shadows of humans: Lakshmana says to Rama, about the demon Viradha: "The anger I felt towards Bharata because he desired the throne, I shall expend on Viradha."[12] Focusing on our central characters, it might be said that Ravana is a shadow of both Rama and Rama's father, Dasharatha. Ravana's epithet of "Ten Necks" (Dashagriva) mirrors the name of Dasharatha ("Ten Chariots")—the demon's is a natural epithet, the human's is a cultural epithet; their characters, too, are similar: both are sex-obsessed. (Similarly the names of Sugriva and Dashagriva connect the monkey and the demon as two natural creatures in contrast with humans.) Like Dasharatha, Ravana is an evil father: because of him, his virtuous son Indrajit is killed. Far more significant, however, is Ravana's role as a shadow of Rama; more precisely, Ravana and his brothers are the shadows of Rama and his brothers. Just as Rama, Lakshmana, and Bharata form a sort of triad (Shatrughna being hardly more than the other half of Lakshmana, and Kubera performing a similarly distant function for Ravana), so too Ravana, Vibhishana, and Kumbhakarna form a triad. In Freudian terms, Ravana is a wonderful embodiment of the ego—proud, selfish, passionate—while Vibhishana, the virtuous demon, who sermonizes Ravana and finally defects to Rama, is pure superego, all conscience and moralizing, and Kumbhakarna, who sleeps for years at a time and wakes only to eat and fight, is a superb literary incarnation of the id: he sleeps and eats (while Ravana takes care of the lust). The triad is even more significant in Indian terms, where they might be viewed as representations of the three constituent strands of matter (called the *gunas*, or qualities): Ravana is *rajas* (energy, passion), Vibhishana *sattva* (lucidity, goodness), and Kumbhakarna *tamas* (entropy, darkness). Ravana remarks, after Kumbhakarna's death, that Kumbhakarna had been his right arm, which is precisely what Rama says of Lakshmana. Ravana also says that Sita is no use to him with Kumbhakarna dead, which is, again, what Rama says when he thinks Lakshmana is dead. But both Vibhishana and Kumbhakarna revile Ravana, in contrast with Lakshmana and Vibhishana who love Rama beyond all credibility.

Turning to the female demons, it is not surprising to find that Sita, too, has a demonic shadow, Ravana's sister, the hideous demoness Shurpanakha. In the Valmiki text, Shurpanakha attempts to seduce Rama and is repulsed by Lakshmana, who cuts off her nose. She tells Ravana about Sita, praising her beauty, and thus triggers the war, just as Sita is said to be its ultimate cause. In Kamban's Tamil version of the *Ramayana*, composed in the twelfth century C. E., Shurpanakha impersonates Sita for Rama, who sees through the trick:

> The demoness Shurpanakha, the sister of Ravana, well aware of her ugliness, fell in love with Rama, who rejected her and instructed his brother to mutilate her by cutting off her nose, ears, and breasts. She then transformed herself into the image of the divine form of Sita. When the real Sita appeared, Shurpanakha told Rama that the other woman [the real Sita] was a deceitful, man-eating demoness who was skilled in the arts of illusion and had adopted a false form. Rama knew who was who but continued to tease Shurpanakha. When Sita ran to Rama and embraced him, Rama rejected Shurpanakha.[13]

The poet makes explicit the demoness's motive; she reasons, "He will never look at me while she who has no equal is near him./ Best for me to run there fast, take her and hide her away somewhere quickly/ and then I will assume that form that he loves and I will live with him."[14] But she does not in fact hide Sita away; the two Sitas, the original and the double, stand there side by side.[15] In the *Balaramayana*, a later retelling, Shurpanakha takes the form of Kaikeyi, and another demon takes the form of Dasharatha, and *they* banish Rama; Dasharatha and Kaikeyi have nothing to do with it at all! Projection here hath made its masterpiece.

Illusory Doubles in the *Ramayana*: the Shadow Sita

The deer that lures Rama away so that Ravana can gain access to Sita is not a real deer: Ravana persuades his pal the demon Maricha to appear as a golden deer to lure Rama and Lakshmana away from protecting Sita, and then he himself appears as an ascetic to lure Sita out of the safe area. From the very start of this episode, Sita is fooled and insists that Rama go after the deer; she is also fooled when the demon mimics Rama's voice calling for help, and she insists Lakshmana go to him, ignoring Lakshmana's wise warning that it is probably just a demonic imitation.[16] Demons, of course, are masters of illusion: Ravana's son produces an illusion of Sita being killed in order to dishearten Rama in the battle,[17] and Ravana attempts, in vain, to bed Sita by producing the illusion of the severed head of her husband; Sita falls for it but grieves without seeking comfort from Ravana, and the illusory head vanishes when Ravana leaves.[18]

In later *Ramayanas*, many more illusory doubles spring up, but by far the most important is the shadow Sita. The fifteenth-century *Adhyatma-ramayana* found it necessary to exculpate Sita not only from being present in Ravana's home but from the weakness of asking Rama to capture the golden deer for her. This illusory deer, however, may have inspired the *Adhyatma-ramayana* to create the illusory Sita who now desires the deer:

> Rama, knowing what Ravana intended to do, told Sita, "Ravana will come to you disguised as an ascetic; put a shadow of yourself outside the hut, and go inside the hut yourself. Live inside fire, invisible, for a year; when I have killed Ravana, come back to me as you were before." Sita obeyed; she placed an illusory Sita (*mayasita*) outside and entered the fire. This illusory Sita saw the illusory deer and urged Rama to capture it for her.[19]

Rama then pretends to grieve for Sita, pretends to fight to get her back, and lies to his brother Lakshmana, who genuinely grieves for Sita. Sita herself is never subjected to an ordeal at all: after Ravana has been killed and the false Sita brought back and accused, the illusory Sita enters the fire and vanishes forever, while the real Sita emerges and remains with Rama.[20] But Rama seems to forget what he has done; he orders the illusory Sita into the fire as if she were real. Probably in order to maintain the power of the narrative, the author has Rama seem to forget about the shadow at crucial moments; only when the gods come and remind him of his divinity (as they do in the Valmiki text) does Fire (incarnate as the god Agni) return Sita to Rama, remarking, "You made this illusory Sita in order to destroy Ravana. Now he is dead, and that Sita has disappeared."[21] Thus Rama creates the shadow but suffers as if he had been helpless to protect his wife. And where Sita's desire for the deer in the Valmiki text proves that she can't recognize a substitute deer, in this text she gets a substitute who can't recognize the substitute deer.

In a later Sanskrit text, the shadow Sita goes on to have a life of her own as a woman notorious for her sexuality:

> One day when Sita and Rama were in the forest, the god of Fire came to Rama, took the true Sita, constructed an illusory shadow Sita, with qualities, form, and limbs equal to hers, and gave her to Rama. He told Rama not

to divulge the secret to anyone; even Rama's brother Lakshmana did not know. Eventually, Rama subjected Sita to the ordeal of fire and Fire restored the real Sita to Rama.

But then the shadow Sita asked Rama and Fire, "What shall I do?" Fire told her to go to the Pushkara shrine, and there she generated inner heat and was reborn as Draupadi. In the Golden Age she is called Vedavati; in the Second Age, she is [the shadow] Sita. And in the Third Age, the shadow is Draupadi. This shadow, who was in the prime of her youth, was so nervous and excited with lust when she asked Shiva for a husband that she repeated her request five times. And so she obtained five husbands, the five Pandavas.[22]

Here it is Fire rather than Rama who constructs the double; Rama has lost some of his agency. And it is Fire who gives the shadow Sita a sexual future; for when she has saved the original Sita from contact with Ravana, she goes on to be reborn as Draupadi, heroine of the other epic, the *Mahabharata*, and of many contemporary cults—a woman with five husbands, unheard of in polygynous, but never polyandrous, Hinduism. Significantly, too, Draupadi, like the shadow Sita in some variants, is born out of a fire; indeed, it may have been this episode in her history that attracted Draupadi from her own epic into Sita's story in the other epic, as if Hamlet somehow popped up as a character in *King Lear*.[23] Or, perhaps, the birth of Draupadi from fire inspired the episode of the birth of the shadow Sita from fire. When the tradition fleshes out the *Ramayana*'s ideologically correct characters, it gives them pre-histories as well as post-histories.

Why so many doubles of Sita? As Rama and Sita become gods, the *bhakti* tradition covers up for them, invoking the double Sita like a *deus ex machina*. The complex doublings of Sita grow in part out of the doctrine of illusion that is woven throughout all *Ramayanas*.[24] But they are also inspired by a deep ambiguity in the attitude to Sita's sexuality. On the one hand, she is the epitome of female chastity. On the other hand, the demoness Shurpanakha is able to double for Sita because both of them are highly sexual women—a quality that may also explain why Ravana is able to carry Sita off in the first place.[25]

As history (in the form of epigraphs and inscriptions, proclamations and panegyrics) claimed the epic for its paradigms, religious texts claimed it all the more for the ahistorical realms of eternity. The Hindus developed the shadow Sita during centuries of occupation by an invasive foreign presence. For, in the twelfth century, the *Ramayana* became a paradigm for a certain sort of history in response to the Turkic presence in India; it began to be used to demonize historical figures, to cast them as actors in the *Ramayana* battle.[26] The battle became a holy war, invoked even in our day (1992, to be more precise) to justify the destruction of the Babri mosque said to stand over Rama's birthplace—an act that triggered riots in which hundreds of Muslims and Hindus were killed.

SUPPLEMENTARY MYTHS: RAVANA AS RAPIST

Over the centuries, Sita's ordeal has proved problematic for different reasons to different South Asians, from pious apologists who were embarrassed by the God's cruelty to his wife, to feminists who saw in Sita's acceptance of the "cool" flames, in Tulsi's telling, and in the connection with Sati, an alarming precedent for suttee, the immolation of widows on their husbands' pyres. Both North and South Indians identified Rama with the North and Ravana with the South; but the North demonized the "Dravidian" Ravana, the South the "Aryan" Rama. And as the *Ramayana* became increasingly problematic, even during the centuries immediately following its recension, another kind of shadowing took place: a number of myths were introduced back into the text as shadows of the central plot.

Many of these myths occur in book 1, a kind of prelude that was most likely an afterthought, probably composed after the other books; others occur in book 7, the last book, which is also probably later than the central 5 books, and, indeed, later than book 1. Though only loosely connected to the plot, these myths set the stage by establishing precedents for some of the irregular behavior that we will encounter once the central story gets under way; their relevance to the main story inspired the storyteller[s] to select them rather than some of the many other myths that were available at that time. The ascetic Rishyashringa, born when his father is aroused by a female antelope, introduces us to intimate contact with animals, preparing us for the lustful monkeys; the demoness Tataka poses a moral dilemma (Should you kill a woman if she is herself a murderess?) that Rama will face with Shurpanakha. Most relevant of all is the story of Ahalya, which tells us the origin of adultery, and tells it twice. Both times, Indra, the king of the gods, seduces Ahalya, the wife of the sage Gautama. The second time, in book 7, Indra simply takes Ahalya by force. Though Gautama curses her for being loose, or unsteady, and led astray by her beauty, the text gives no evidence of this. The fact that she was raped should, we might assume, absolve Ahalya of any misdoing: she was helpless. But this argument is never made; perhaps these ancient texts already assumed, like modern sexists, that any woman who is raped is asking for it. When Ravana rapes Rambha—in a story we are about to consider—he is referred to as a "demonic Indra," and the *Kamasutra* singles out Indra with Ahalya and Ravana with Sita as examples of men who were destroyed by uncontrolled desire.[27] Clearly Indra is behaving in a demonic manner. The first time the story is told, in book 1, Indra uses another technique that links him with Ravana: illusion. Indra takes the form of Gautama, but by merely putting on the sage's clothing; Ahalya immediately recognizes him but willingly goes to bed with him, "because she was sexually curious about the king of the gods." Gautama curses her to become invisible; Sita too was rendered invisible when she was merely vulnerable to a rape. The complexities of the tale of Ahalya with Indra nuance and to some extent problematize the parallel but not identical complexities of the tale of Sita with Ravana.

But that story, too, has explicit multiple variants, one of which is in the last book, the book of afterthoughts. Rama banishes Sita twice (just as Indra seduces Ahalya twice); the first time, in book 6, Sita goes into the fire but comes back again; the second time, in book 7, she plunges down into the earth, her mother, and does not come back again. Was there something unsatisfactory about the first banishment? Clearly there was, as it inspired all those doubles to go into the fire in Sita's place. Perhaps it also inspired some poet to add on another, more final and more noble exit for Sita. Book 7 also resolves a puzzle, closely related to the puzzle of Rama's banishment of Sita, that must have troubled readers and hearers: why does Ravana not rape Sita? When Ravana carries Sita off, he tries to seduce her with words and threats, but never by force. Why not? The author of book 7 explains Ravana's reticence by citing a curse put upon him after his rape of Rambha:

> One day, when Ravana was full of passion, he saw the celestial courtesan Rambha and went mad with lust for her. She reminded him that she was his daughter-in-law, more precisely the wife of Nalakubara, the son of his brother Vaishravana. But Ravana replied, "You say you are my daughter-in-law. For those who have but one husband, this argument is valid, but in their world the gods have established a law said to be eternal, that celestial courtesans have no appointed consorts, nor are the gods monogamous." Then he raped her. When he released her she ran home, trembling with fear, and told her husband, who said, "Since he raped you brutally, despite your lack of desire for him, he will never be able to approach another young woman unless she shares his desire. If, carried away by lust, he does violence to any woman who does not desire him, his head will split

into seven pieces." When Ravana learned of the curse his hair stood on end and he ceased to indulge in uniting himself with those who had no desire for him. And the chaste married women whom he had raped rejoiced when they heard this curse.[28]

And that's why Ravana never raped Sita. A Tibetan text of uncertain provenance states that when Sita sent Lakshmana after Rama she not only accused him of having designs on her but added a curse: "Perhaps the younger brother thinks in his mind that, when the elder brother is dead, he will live together with me. If I do not want it, then, let whoever will touch me be burned."[29] And it was this curse, uttered by Sita herself, that protected her, not against the innocent Lakshmana but against Ravana, who when he arrived "knew that, if he touched the queen, he would be burned." Sita herself here assumes one aspect of the role of Rambha: she curses her rapist, unknowingly projecting upon her future assailant, the demon Ravana, a punishment designed for her present non-assailant, the human Lakshmana.

Later *Ramayanas* speculated on the reasons why, if Ravana could fool Sita by taking on the form of a Brahmin sage, he could not seduce her by taking on the form of Rama. A Bengali text tells us:

> Someone said to Ravana, "You are taking various magic forms in order to get Sita. Why don't you take the form of Rama sometime and then approach Sita?" Ravana said, "When I think of Rama and even the realm of *brahman* seems a trifling thing, how could I think of such a trifling thing as another man's wife? And so how can I take the form of Rama?"[30]

Ravana is saying that when he thinks of becoming Rama, already he thinks *like Rama*, and so he can't carry out a dirty trick like pretending to be Rama. Ravana cannot switch into Rama's form because he would get Rama's mind and memory traces along with his form. He would stop being Ravana—and, presumably, paradoxically, stop wanting to change into Rama. So, too, a twelfth-century commentary on poems of devotion to Vishnu argues that if Ravana would take the form of Rama, he would become virtuous, since Rama is the very incarnation of virtue, *dharma*; even if he merely pretended to be virtuous, he would be infected by *dharma*.[31] William Buck expands upon this theme in his English translation, when one of the demons suggests to Ravana, "Take Rama's form by magic, go to Sita, and she will willingly love you." To this Ravana replies, "No, I can't. The transformation would have to be complete; I'd have to take on all Rama's virtues as well to fool her, and then I could do no wrong, I couldn't lie to her and say I was someone I wasn't."[32]

JALANDHARA AS RAVANA, VRINDA AS TULSI

Ravana's fate in the *Ramayana* is developed in yet other ways in other texts, in both Sanskrit and vernacular languages, that link him with the worship of the Tulsi plant, the sacred basil, a central ingredient in the worship of Vishnu. It all begins with the story of the demon Jalandhara, who is born of Shiva alone and tries to seduce his father's wife, Parvati (regarded as his mother):

> Jalandhara reigned with justice, but he usurped the prerogatives of the gods. They asked the sage Narada to help them, and he went to Jalandhara and inspired in him the desire to abduct Parvati. Jalandhara sent an emissary to Shiva asking him to give up Parvati; instead, a great battle ensued, in the course of which Jalandhara created the magic illusion of celestial courtesans. While Shiva was fascinated by the courtesans, Jalandhara, driven by lust, went to the palace where Parvati lived. With his power of illusion he assumed the form of Shiva, with ten arms, five faces, three eyes, and matted hair, seated on the great bull—in every way the image of Shiva. When Parvati saw Shiva approaching, she was full of love for her beloved; she came forward to meet him. But then, realizing that he was a demon, Parvati disappeared immediately, and Jalandhara returned to the battle.[33]

Another retelling introduces another double: Parvati gets her friend Jaya to impersonate her while Jalandhara impersonates Shiva, and even produces a mirage of Shiva carrying the severed heads of her sons Ganesha and Skanda. Still she sees through him. Then, in revenge for this failed seduction, Shiva gets Vishnu to attempt (this time successfully) to seduce Jalandhara's wife, Vrinda, *not* (the text keeps reminding us) out of lust, but because the demon is protected by his wife's fidelity to her husband. Several texts insist upon the tit-for-tat nature of the counter-seduction; in one, as soon as Parvati has penetrated Jalandhara's disguise, she summons Vishnu, tells him what has happened, and demands: "He himself has shown the path: destroy the *dharma* of fidelity of *his* wife. There is no other way for the great demon to be killed, for there is no *dharma* on the face of the earth equal to the fidelity of a wife."[34] Sometimes it is Vishnu himself who says this.[35] In any case, this is what he does:

> Deceiving his wife, Lakshmi, Vishnu used his yogic power of illusion to assume another form, for he was deluded by passion for Vrinda. He gave Vrinda nightmares, portending her own widowhood: she saw the severed head of Jalandhara, its eyes plucked out by a vulture. She awoke and entered a terrible forest; suddenly

she realized that the female mules pulling her chariot had stopped neighing, and that the wheels made no sound, nor the bells. Then a horrible demon devoured the mules, seized Vrinda, and said, "Shiva has killed your husband in the battle, or so I have heard. Take me for your husband and drink sweet wine and eat the meat of large animals." When she heard that, the life went out of her.

Vishnu then appeared in the form of an ascetic, wearing bark garments, and reduced the demon to ashes. Vrinda, fooled by Vishnu's illusory power, threw her arms around Vishnu's neck, a touch which gave him much pleasure, and he said to her, "By your embrace, the head of your husband will come back again, and all his limbs, even better than before." She lay down on the divine bed and picked up the head of her husband and drank kisses from his lower lip and closed her eyes in waves of pleasure. Then Jalandhara seemed to appear, for Vishnu had taken on a handsome form just like his, with his chest, his height, his speech, his frame of mind. Seeing the full form of her beloved, Vrinda cried out, "I will do whatever pleases you, my master. Tell me about the battle." Vishnu-as-Jalandhara said, "My darling, Shiva cut off my head, but just then by your power of yoga, the severed head was brought here and revived by the touch of your body." Then Vrinda, lusting for sexual pleasure, embraced him closely and kissed him. Vishnu thought that the pleasure that came from deluding Vrinda was greater than the delicious pleasure of the love of his wife Lakshmi, and that this sexual release was greater than the pleasure of metaphysical Release. He enjoyed Vrinda's body for a number of days, and then he thought about what he was supposed to do for Shiva.

One day, at the end of their love-making, Vrinda saw Vishnu in his own form, with his two arms around her neck. She loosened the noose of his arms from her neck and said, "How is it that you came to delude me in the form of an ascetic?" And he said, to calm her down, "I am the beloved of Lakshmi. Your husband went to seduce Parvati in order to conquer Shiva, and I am Shiva, and he is me. Jalandhara has been killed in the battle. Make love with me now." Furious, she cursed him, and then she said to her friend, "The sight of my beloved was just an object of the senses made of my own longings." And she killed herself and went to heaven.[36]

Where Jalandhara's trick fails, Vishnu's trick succeeds—or, rather, succeeds long enough for him to seduce the woman he desires. What success he achieves is due in part to his greater skill as a magician: he mimics not only Jalandhara's chest, height, and speech (and, presumably, his multiple arms, which distinguish him from the anthropomorphic, two-armed form of Vishnu) but his "frame of mind." The assumption that you take on another person's morals as well as his social role when you take on his form is not shared by most myths of masquerade. In the prevalent pattern, the demon— such as Jalandhara—merely assumes the outer form of the person he impersonates, retaining his own essence, his memory and mentality. Jalandhara does not feel or think or remember like Shiva; he just looks like him. But these variants of the stories of Vishnu with Vrinda and Ravana with Sita seem to reflect the very opposite view: the masquerader is entirely transformed into someone else, with the mentality and memory of that other person. We might see an equally unexpected inversion of this phenomenon in the late text in which the shadow substituting for Sita goes on to have a kind of subjectivity, this time not Sita's but her own.

Yet another instance of this pattern occurs when Vishnu is ultimately exposed, after love-making, perhaps because his motives turn out not to be so pure after all, for he falls in love with Vrinda just as Jalandhara falls for Parvati. That is, Vishnu actually *becomes* the person whose mask he assumes: a person who is in love with Vrinda. He does not take on Jalandhara's memory or sense of self; he knows that he is Vishnu pretending to be Jalandhara. But gradually he forgets that it is just a game. He becomes his mask. He then justifies the transformation (Vishnu = Jalandhara) by translating it into a theological equation (Vishnu = Shiva); if the gods are one, what does it matter if a woman sleeps with her husband or one god or another?

The textual convention demands that Vishnu succeed at least long enough to let Shiva win the fight: demons must fail, gods must win. Where Jalandhara's trick with death (the mirage of Parvati's dead sons) was anti-erotic, Vishnu's trick with death (the mirage of Jalandhara's corpse and the rejoining of the severed head) is erotic: Vrinda is so happy to see him alive again that she doesn't look too closely. Some of Jalandhara's tricks are stolen straight out of the Valmiki *Ramayana*. Jalandhara produces an illusion of celestial courtesans (*apsarases*)[37] and of Parvati[38] to distract Shiva, just as Ravana's son produces an illusion of Sita being killed in order to dishearten Rama in the battle.[39] Jalandhara produces the severed heads of Parvati's sons in his vain attempt to seduce her, and Vishnu produces an illusion of Jalandhara's corpse in his successful attempt to seduce Vrinda,[40] just as Ravana attempts, in vain, to bed Sita by producing the illusion of the severed head of her husband.[41]

From the start, Vishnu admits that he prefers Vrinda to his own wife, whom he deceives, and even after he is exposed, he tries to persuade Vrinda to go on making love with him. In a variant recorded in Kangra in 1995, Vishnu takes the form of Jalandhara and is brought to Jalandhara's wife (here already called Tulsi, not Vrinda) as a wounded body; when she lifts the body to tend it, she has touched a man other than her husband, and the protection she was giving Jalandhara vanishes.[42] And in a variant recorded in Central India in 1975, Vrinda doesn't even touch the body; she just has to *say* that it is her husband, and that suffices to seal his doom.[43] Several texts address a problem that remains after the fight between Shiva and Jalandhara (or Parvati and Vrinda) has come to an end: Vishnu remains in love with Vrinda, who becomes reincarnate as the Tulsi plant, regarded as a wife of Vishnu and worshipped in conjunction with Vishnu (as the *shalagrama* stone).[44]

The love of Vishnu for Vrinda is an important theme in the later mythology and ritual of Rama.[45] The textual history comes full circle when Vrinda curses Vishnu, saying that someone else disguised as an ascetic will abduct his own wife—that is, that Ravana, disguised as an ascetic, will abduct Sita when Vishnu becomes incarnate as Rama (in the story told in the *Ramayana*). Indeed, Jalandhara becomes reincarnated as Ravana to take away Sita in Tulsi Das's sixteenth century Hindi version of the *Ramayana*, the *Ramacaritamanasa*. When Vrinda curses Vishnu (here called Hari or the Lord), the text says: "By a stratagem the Lord broke her marriage vow and thus accomplished the purpose of the gods. When the lady discovered the deception, she cursed him in her wrath. Hari, the Blessed Lord, sportive and gracious, accepted her curse. It was this Jalandhara who was reborn as Ravana."[46] What was "the stratagem"? One translator, W. D. P. Hill, explains in a helpful footnote: "Vishnu took the form of Jalandhara and approached Vrinda, who at once ceased to pray, with the result that Jalandhara fell down dead."[47] Ceased to *pray*? This English scholar takes us a long way from the Sanskrit and Hindi texts. Thus the *Ramayana* tradition continues to reinvent itself, creating a running commentary on the story and reinserting that commentary inside the text, first within the Sanskrit text of Valmiki and again in every new retelling, for over two thousand years.

WENDY DONIGER
University of Chicago

NOTES

1. Paula Richman, ed. *Many Ramayanas: The Diversity of Narrative Traditions in South Asia* (Berkeley: University of California Press, 1991).

2. *Ramayana* of Valmiki, Critical Edition (Baroda: Oriental Institute, 1960–75), 6.103–6; Wendy Doniger O'Flaherty, *Dreams, Illusion, and Other Realities* (Chicago: University of Chicago Press, 1984), 92; Wendy Doniger O'Flaherty, *Hindu Myths* (Harmondsworth: Penguin, 1975), 198–204. I have for the most part translated the Sanskrit rather freely and given no footnotes, but occasionally, where a more precise wording was required, I have been more precise and supplied the precise source in the note.

3. *Ramayana* 2.71.13.

4. Robert Goldman, "Rama Sahalaksmanah: Psychological and Literary Aspects of the Composite Hero in Valmiki's *Ramayana*," *Journal of Indian Philosophy* 8 (1980), 149–89.

5. *The Laws of Manu* [*Manusmrti*], ed. Harikrishna Jayantakrishna Dave (Bombay: Bharatiya Vidya Series, vol. 29 ff., 1972–8), trans. Wendy Doniger, with Brian K. Smith (Harmondsworth: Penguin Books, 1991), 9.60; Wendy Doniger, *The Bedtrick: Tales of Sex and Masquerade* (Chicago: University of Chicago Press, 2000), chapter 6.

6. *Kamasutra* of Vatsyayana (with the commentary of Yashodhara), ed. with the Hindi "Jaya" commentary by Devadatta Shastri, Kashi Sanskrit Series 29 (Chaukhambha Sanskrit Sansthan, Varanasi, 1964), 5.1:53.

7. *Ramayana* 2.80.10.

8. J. L. Masson, "Fratricide and the Monkeys: Psychoanalytic Observations on an Episode in the Valmikiramayanam," *Journal of the American Oriental Society* 95 (1975): 454–59.

9. Sugriva is the son of Surya (the Sun god); Valin is the son of Indra (king of the gods, god of rain); and Hanuman, the great general of Sugriva's army, is the son of Vayu, the wind. In this, the monkeys particularly resemble the human heroes of the other great Sanskrit epic, the *Mahabharata*, in which Surya is the father of Karna, Indra the father of Arjuna, and Vayu the father of Bhima.

10. Gary Saul Morson, *Narrative and Freedom: The Shadows of Time* (New Haven and London: Yale University Press, 1994).

11. See the story of Mayiliravana, told in O'Flaherty, *Dreams, Illusion, and Other Realities*.

12. *Ramayana* 3.2.26.

13. Kamban, *Ramayana*, 2888–2891, in George Hart and Hank Heifetz, trans., *The Forest Book of the Ramayana* [of Kamban] (Berkeley: University of California Press, 1988).

14. Kamban *Ramayana* 2918; Hart, *The Forest Book*.

15. See Wendy Doniger, *Splitting the Difference: Gender and Myth in Ancient Greece and India* (Chicago: University of Chicago Press, 1999).

16. *Ramayana* 3.42.14; 3.43.1–10, 21–23.

17. *Ramayana* 6.68.1–28.

18. *Ramayana* 6.31.

19. *Adhyatma-ramayana*, with the commentaries of Narottama, Ramavarman, and Gopala Chakravarti, Calcutta Sanskrit series, no. 11 (Calcutta: Metropolitan Printing & Publishing House, 1935), 3.7.1–10.
20. There may be an ancient connection between the myth of Sita protected by fire and the Norse myth of Brunnhilde, whose virginity is protected when her father puts her to sleep within a circle of fire.
21. *Adhyatma-Ramayana* 6.8.21.
22. *Brahmavaivarta Purana* (Poona: Anandashrama Sanskrit Series #102, 1935) 2.14.1–59.
23. *Mahabharata*, Critical Edition (Poona: Bhandarkar Oriental Research Institute, 1933-69), 1.175.
24. O'Flaherty, *Dreams*, 92–97.
25. David Dean Shulman, "Sita and Satakantharavana in a Tamil Folk Narrative," *Journal of Indian Folkloristics* 2 (1979): 12–16.
26. Sheldon Pollock, "*Ramayana* and Political Imagination in India," *Journal of Asian Studies* 52:2 (May, 1993): 261–297.
27. *Kamasutra* 1.2.36.
28. *Ramayana* 7.26.8–47, plus the verses excised from the Critical Edition after verses 30 and 47. See Doniger, *Splitting the Difference*.
29. J. W. de Jong, *The Story of Rama in Tibet: Text and Translation of the Tun-huang Manuscripts* (Stuttgart: Franz Steiner Verlag, 1989), 153–62.
30. *Shrishriramakrishnakathamrita* 1.181, trans. Jeffrey Kripal, personal communication, May, 1993. *Tuccham brahmapadam paravadhusangah kutah.*
31. Acharya K. V. Raman, personal communication, Madras, January 1996.
32. William Buck, *Ramayana* (Berkeley: University of California Press, 1976), 301.
33. *Shiva Purana* (Benares: Pandita Pustakalaya, 1964), 2.5.13–22; cf. *Padma Purana* (Poona, Anandashrama Sanskrit Series 131, 1893), 6.97–103; Doniger, *The Bedtrick*.
34. *Shiva Purana* 2.5.22.
35. *Padma Purana* 6.102.29.
36. *Padma Purana* 6.15–16; cf. *Shiva Purana* 2.5.22–24.
37. *Shiva Purana* 2.5.22; cf. *Padma Purana* 6.97–103.
38. *Padma Purana* 6.19.14–45; cf. *Shiva Purana* 2.5.24.
39. *Ramayana* 6.68.1–28.
40. *Padma Purana* 6.15–16.
41. *Ramayana* 6.31.
42. Kirin Narayan, "The Tulsi Plant in Kangra," ms. forthcoming.
43. Lawrence Babb, *The Divine Hierarchy: Popular Hinduism in Central India* (New York and London: Columbia University Press, 1975), 107–8.
44. *Shiva Purana* 2.5.26.46–52; cf. *Padma Purana* 6.105.1–7.
46. *Brahmavaivarta Purana* 2.15–21.
47. Tulsidas, *The Holy Lake*, trans. R. C. Prasad (Delhi: Motilal Banarsidass, 1990), 1.124.
47 Tulsi Das, *Ramacaritamanasa*, trans. W. D. P. Hill (London: Oxford University Press, 1952), 512.

Translations of Various Ramayanas

Of Valmiki's Sanskrit Text

Buck, William. *Ramayana.* abridged version. Berkeley: University of California Press, 1976.

Goldman, Robert P. ed. *The Ramayana: An Epic of Ancient India.* 5 vols. incomplete. Princeton, N.J.: Princeton University Press: 1984–1996.

Raghunathan, N. trans. *Srimad Valmiki Ramayana.* 3 vols. complete. Madras: Vighneswara Publishing House, 1981–1982.

Sattar, Arshia, trans. *The Ramayana.* excerpts. New Delhi: Viking Penguin, 1996.

Shastri, Hari Prasad, trans. *The Ramayana.* 3 vols. complete. rev. ed. London: Shanti Sadan, 1962.

Swami Venkatesananda. *The Concise Ramayana of Valmiki.* abridged version. Albany: State University of New York Press, 1988.

Of Kampan's Tamil Text

Hart, George and Heifetz, Hank, trans. *The Forest Book of the Ramayana [of Kamban].* Book 1. Berkeley: University of California Press, 1988.

Narayan, R. K. *The Ramayana.* abridged version. New York: Viking Press, 1972.

Of Tulsi's Hindi Text

Tulsidas, *The Holy Lake.* Trans. R. C. Prasad. Delhi: Motilal Banarsidass, 1990.

Tulsidas, *Ramacaritamanasa.* Trans. W. D. P. Hill. London: Oxford University Press, 1952.

Other Ramayanas

Adhyatmaramayana. Trans. Rai Bahadur Nala Baij Nath. Allahabad: The Sacred Books of the Hindus, the Panini Office, 1913.

de Jong, J. W. *The Story of Rama in Tibet: Text and Translation of the Tun-huang Manuscripts.* Stuttgart: Franz Steiner Verlag, 1989.

Suggestions for Further Reading

Brockington, John. *The Sanskrit Epics.* Leiden: Koninklijke Brill, 1998.

Doniger, Wendy. *Splitting the Difference: Gender and Myth in Ancient Greece and India.* Chicago: University of Chicago Press, 1999.

Goldman, Robert. "Rama Sahalaksmanah: Psychological and Literary Aspects of the Composite Hero in Valmiki's Ramayana." *Journal of Indian Philosophy* 8 (1980): 149–89.

Lutgendorf, Philip. *The Life of a Text: Performing the Ramcaritmanas of Tulsidas.* Berkeley: University of California Press, 1991.

Masson, J. L. "Fratricide and the Monkeys: Psychoanalytic Observations on an Episode in the *Valmikiramayanam.*" *Journal of the American Oriental Society* 95 (1975): 454–59.

Menen, Aubrey. *The Ramayana.* New York: Scribner, 1954.

Pollock, Sheldon. "*Ramayana* and Political Imagination in India." *Journal of Asian Studies* 52:2 (May, 1993): 261–297.

Richman, Paula, ed. *Many Ramayanas: The Diversity of Narrative Traditions in South Asia.* Berkeley: University of California Press, 1991.

Richman, Paula, ed. *Questioning Ramayanas: A South Asian Tradition.* Berkeley: University of California Press, 2001.

Shulman, David Dean. "Sita and Satakantharavana in a Tamil Folk Narrative." *Journal of Indian Folkloristics* 2 [1979]: 1–26.

Discussion Questions

In King Rama, we encounter an epic hero who is clearly to some extent deified, especially by the later tradition. In what sense exactly is Rama divine? Does this make him omniscient, infallible, omnipotent? In what ways does the text specifically support—or undercut—the view of Rama as a god or God?

Valmiki populates the world of his epic with creatures of all sorts and with three main forms of society—humans, monkeys, and rakshasas. How does the co-presence of these alternate communities influence how we understand each one?

The theme of forced exile sets the stage for the *Ramayana*'s dramatic action, as it does in certain other epics as well. What is the essential cause of his exile? Who is responsible? What is the significance of such forced exile in the case of the god-man, Rama?

How are we meant to understand the forcible abduction of Sita by Ravana? Who is ultimately to blame? Ravana? Shurpanakha? Lakshmana? Rama? Sita? Dasharatha?

What is the narrative significance of the long digression in the midst of the story about the feud between Sugriva and his brother Vali? How does it relate to the main narrative?

Characters of this narrative—whether human beings, monkeys, or rakshasas—repeatedly and piously invoke the authority of dharma at crucial points throughout the story. How does Valmiki lead us to understand dharma in this narrative? Is it always necessarily synonymous with the authority and behavior of Lord Rama? If not, why not?

What is the narrative structure of the *Ramayana*? What do you make of the liberal use of multiple narrators, frame stories (such as the story of Narada's response to Valmiki), or inset stories (such as the digression about the sons of Sagara and the descent of the river Ganges)?

In later tradition, Sita is generally conceived as the paragon of the ideal Hindu wife, yet she is also believed to be a goddess "born from the furrow of the earth." How does Valmiki's account depict the character of Sita—simple or complex, powerless or powerful, goddess or victim? And what do you make of her apparent connection to the Earth and Fire?

How would you explain—could you defend—Rama's apparently mean-spirited repudiation of Sita, not once but twice at the end of Valmiki's narrative?

In later tradition, Hanuman also assumes the status of a god. How do you understand Hanuman's role and activity in the *Ramayana*? Is he a quintessential monkey or does he in some ways transcend his monkey status?

Discussion Points

• The boundaries and distinctions between human beings and other creatures, e.g., monkeys, rakshasas, devas, etc.

• The role of dharma in the epic and its relation to Lord Rama.

• Meaning and significance of Rama's identity as a god or God.

• The relation between the narrative and the real or imagined topography of India.

•Ways in which the narrative has been informed by religious and philosophical doctrines native to India, such as reincarnation and rebirth, the power of asceticism, the role of illusion, the caste system, and the existence of dharma.

• The apparent development and structure of the Valmiki *Ramayana*.

• Parallels between the human society and the society of the rakshasas and monkeys.

• Episodes of illusion, deception, disguise, or masquerade.

Points for Further Investigation

• The relationship between books 1 and 7, and the rest of Valmiki's narrative.

• Literary aspects of the narrative, in particular the place of the *Ramayana*, characterized as the first of poems (*adikavya*), in the tradition of Sanskrit poetry and poetics.

• Historical and literary relationship between the *Ramayana* and the *Mahabharata*.

• The use of particular narrative strategies, such as frame and inset stories, by Valmiki.

• Ways in which later retellings of the Rama story come to terms with Rama's repudiation of Sita at the end.

• The role of sexual desire and its relation to chastity in the epic.

- The relationship between dharma and devotion to Rama.
- Role of the doctrine of divine descent or incarnation (*avatara*) in the *Ramayana*.
- The impact of mantras, oaths, and curses, and the view of language they presuppose.

TÁIN

The last of the ancient texts we will consider in this volume, the *Táin Bó Cúailnge* ("The Cattle-Raid of Cooley") comes to us from the Celtic traditions of ancient Ireland. Though first recorded mainly in prose, not poetry, probably by Irish monks sometime between the seventh and the ninth century of the Common Era, this narrative reflects the existence of a lively oral tradition stretching as far back as the first century B.C.E., when the incidents it recounts might well have actually taken place. A central text in the Ulster cycle of stories, the *Táin* relates the misadventures of the armies of Connacht and their allies, under the command of the mercurial Queen Medb, in their ill-advised invasion of the northern province of Ulster in order to carry off the famed Brown Bull of Cúailnge. The hero of the story is a young Ulster warrior named Cú Chulainn ("the Hound of Culann"), a ferocious mountain of a man, who despite his young age, single-handedly holds off the armies of Connacht and the "Men of Ireland" until the Ulster warriors can recover from their annual winter torpor and rally to their own defense. In his essay, noted Celtic scholar, Tomás Ó Cathasaigh offers us a glimpse into the ties of kinship and family loyalty that knit together these warrior societies and inspired their most dramatic acts of militant heroism.

Táin Timeline

8000–7000	Earliest human habitation of Ireland—mesolithic hunters and fishers
4000	Arrival of New Stone Age people—farmers and megaligthic builders
2500–500	Irish Bronze Age
700	Arrival of Celtic settlers
5c	Early Iron Age—Hallstatt influence
387	Celts sack Rome
3c	La Tène artifacts and cultural traditions
B.C.E.	
C.E.	
1c	All Celtic territories under Roman rule, except for Ireland and Scottish Highlands
	Traditional Age of the heroes
432	Traditional date of Patrick's return to Ireland
400	Ulster Cycle
7–9c	*Táin*—Recension I
795	First Viking invasion
1014	Defeat of Vikings at the Battle of Clontarf
12c	*Táin*—Recension II
1167–1169	Norman Invasion of Ireland
1171	Henry II visits and claims Ireland

ANCIENT IRELAND

TÁIN BÓ CÚAILINGE

> "Every man has kindly feelings for his own people."
> (197; K 170)

Táin Bó Cúailnge 'The Cattle-Raid of Cooley', often referred to simply as the *Táin*, tells of an invasion of Ulster by a great army led by Medb and her husband, Ailill, who is king of Connacht (in the north-west of Ireland); its purpose is to carry off the Brown Bull from the Cooley peninsula in what is now County Louth (in the north-east). Medb is the instigator of the raid, and hers is one of the strongest and most insistent voices in the tale. I shall be attending to some of her utterances in what follows, and the words of hers which I have used as epigraph point to the theme of love of one's kindred which will be the primary focus of what I wish to say today about the *Táin*. When the mighty army assembled by Medb and Ailill are about to set out from their court at Rathcroghan, Medb displays an acute awareness of what she has taken upon herself when she says to her charioteer: "'All those who part here today from comrade and friend will curse me for it is I who has mustered this hosting'" (126; K 60).[1] It is typical of Medb that she does not allow this insight to influence her actions in any way. As her ill-fated enterprise proceeds, her words as well as her deeds expose her as the arrogant, heartless, dishonest, cynical—and endlessly fascinating—manipulator that she is. Her character is of course revealed cumulatively, but here perhaps one example will suffice to show the kind of person we are dealing with. In the course of the invasion, Medb and Ailill are obliged to seek one warrior after another who will be brave (or foolhardy) enough to face the apparently invincible Cú Chulainn in single combat, since for a long time he is the only one who stands between the invaders and the achievement of their goal. When it has been decided that a certain Cúr mac Da Lath should be asked to take on this task, Medb remarks: "'If he kill Cú Chulainn it means victory. If he is himself killed, it will be a relief to the host. It is not pleasant to consort with Cúr eating and sleeping'" (172; K 127). She seems to feel that the death of the individual who continues to thwart them is of no greater moment than ridding themselves of the hapless Cúr, one of their own warriors, whose table manners and sleeping habits are not to her liking.

Medb remains her wayward and irrepressible self through all the vicissitudes of the raid until, at last, her allies desert her, and her army is vanquished. She then finds herself at Cú Chulainn's mercy, and all she can do is utter the simple and humble words

"Spare me!" (236; K 250). Cú Chulainn lets her know that she deserves to die, but he does spare her. Her last, brief, words are to Fergus: they are evidently an admission of defeat—the tentative translation is "'Men and lesser men (?) meet here today, Fergus'" (236; K 251). In any case, Fergus issues a stunning rebuke: "'That is what usually happens to a herd of horses led by a mare. Their substance is taken and carried off and guarded as they follow a woman who has misled them'" (237; K 251). She is reduced to silence, and even the subsequent contest of the bulls, which is watched by all the survivors of the battle, draws no comment from her.

The *Táin* begins with the mustering of an army, which is so great that it is often referred to as "the men of Ireland." As they are about to set out on the raid, and just after Medb has predicted that she will be cursed by the troops, she meets the prophetess Feidelm, who warns her that her expedition will be a bloody one. Medb comforts herself in the knowledge that the Ulster king Conchobor "'lies in his debility in Emain together with the Ulstermen and all the mightiest of their warriors'" (126; K 61). This "debility" is one to which adult Ulstermen are peculiarly prone; it lasts for "the three months of winter"—from the first of November to the first of February—and during that time they are too weak to engage in the defense of their province. There is, however, one young man living in Ulster who is not stricken with the debility: this is of course Cú Chulainn ("The Hound of Culann"), and the reason for his immunity is that his kinship with the Ulstermen is through his mother—his father Súaltaim is also immune from the debility. Cú Chulainn greatly impedes the invaders as they make their way across the country, but they do eventually reach Finnabair in Cooley and from there they "spread out over the province [of Ulster] in quest of the Bull" (128; K 65). They are unsuccessful at first: "the army scattered and set the country on fire. They gathered all the women, boys, girls and cows that were in Cooley and brought them all to Findabair" (152; K 100), but they did not find the bull. Having harried Cooley, the army goes southward to Conaille, driving the cattle before them. When they arrive in Conaille, Cú Chulainn kills so many of them that Ailill makes terms with him. It is agreed that each day Cú Chulainn will engage a warrior in single combat at a ford, and that in the meantime the army will not take the cattle away (160; K 117). Cú Chulainn vanquishes a great number of opponents in this way; and even when the invaders capture the bull and take it into their encampment (167; K 126), Cú Chulainn remains as an obstacle in their path. A small number of Cú Chulainn's combats are described in detail, culminating in the killing of his beloved foster-brother, Fer Diad.

The cattle-raid leads ultimately to a great battle between Connacht and Ulster, but owing to the debility of the Ulstermen, the warfare between the provinces is asymmetrical: we begin with the muster of the Connachta and their allies, and we do not reach the muster of the Ulstermen until more than three-fourths of the tale has been told (218; K 220). Somewhat earlier, as the three months of winter come to an end, individual Ulstermen begin to recover their vigor, and they come to challenge the invaders. When the Ulstermen are finally free of the debility, they muster a huge force and meet and vanquish the Connachta in the great battle.

This asymmetry in the *Táin* is what calls Cú Chulainn to the single-handed defense of Ulster: the temporary disablement of the men of Ulster requires (and allows) him to assume the role of an epic hero. That Cú Chulainn is destined for greatness is already clear in the story of his birth. This is told, not in the *Táin*, but in one of the 'prefatory' or 'preliminary' tales (Irish *remscéla*) associated with it, and which inform us about some of the personages in the *Táin* and help us to understand the circumstances in which they find themselves. The story of Cú Chulainn's birth is a variation on a common heroic pattern, and shows him to have a divine father, Lug, as well as a human father, Súaltaim. Each of them, as we shall see, is assigned a role in the *Táin*. Cú Chulainn is a precocious hero, as the invaders soon discover. While they are still in the initial stages of their journey from Connacht to Cooley, Fergus sends a warning of the forthcoming invasion to the Ulstermen. This is received by Cú Chulainn and Súaltaim. They go to watch out for the invaders, and Cú Chulainn has a premonition that they will arrive that very night. This poses a difficulty for him, as he has an assignation with a woman, which he is honor-bound to keep. He takes elaborate (and successful) steps to delay the invaders while he goes to meet his lover. Medb and Ailill are curious to know more about the formidable foe who has contrived to stop them in their tracks, and it is in that context that we are given "The Eulogy of Cú Chulainn" and the long section devoted to his "Boyhood Deeds."

By way of introduction to "The Eulogy," and in response to a question from Ailill, Fergus says of Cú Chulainn: "'In his fifth year he went to the boys in Emain Macha to play. In his sixth year he went to learn feats of arms to Scáthach and went to woo Emer. In his seventh year he took up arms. At the present time he is seventeen years old'" (135; K 75). Medb then asks, "'Is he the most formidable among the Ulstermen?'" and this elicits the following eulogy:

> "More so than any of them," answered Fergus. "You will not encounter a warrior harder to deal with, nor a spear-point sharper or keener or quicker, nor a hero fiercer, nor a raven more voracious, nor one of his age to equal a third of his valour, nor a lion more savage, nor a shelter in battle nor a sledge-hammer for smiting, nor a protector in fighting, nor doom of hosts, nor one better able to check a great army. You will not find there any man his equal in age like unto Cú Chulainn in growth, in dress, in fearsomeness, in speech, in splendour, in voice and appearance, in power and harshness, in feats, in valour, in striking power, in rage and in anger, in victory and in doom-dealing and in violence, in stalking, in sureness of aim and in game-killing, in swiftness and boldness and rage, with the feat of nine men on every spear-point." (135; K 75)

I thought it was worth quoting this in full, partly to compensate for the fact that I will not have a lot to say about Cú Chulainn's extraordinary feats in the *Táin*, which vindicate Fergus's florid tribute, but mainly because otherwise it would be difficult to appreciate the sheer audacity of Medb's response: "'I reck little of that,' said Medb. 'He has but one body; he suffers wounding; he is not beyond capture. Moreover he is only the age of a grown girl and as yet his manly deeds have not developed.'" The notion that Cú Chulainn is not yet ready for his task is contested by Fergus: "'Nay,' said Fergus. 'It were no wonder that he should perform a goodly exploit today, for even when he was younger, his deeds were those of a man'" (136; K 76). He then launches into an account of the first of Cú Chulainn's "Boyhood Deeds," telling how he went to join the boys in Emain Macha, an episode to which, as we have seen, Fergus has already briefly alluded.

In her curt dismissal of Fergus's words, Medb seriously underestimates the hero, disregarding the evidence of her eyes and ears. It is of course literally true that Cú Chulainn has but one body, and while he is never captured, he is grievously wounded in the *Táin*. The full extent of Medb's misjudgment becomes clear only as the raid progresses, but it is already about to be adumbrated in "The Boyhood Deeds." These episodes from Cú Chulainn's childhood and youth show him arriving, unbidden, at Emain Macha, and his gradual incorporation into Ulster society. The feats that he performs as he goes through successive stages of initiation into warrior status show how well fitted he is for the role that befalls him in the *Táin*. Most dramatically, we discover that his containment within that "one body" of his is sometimes alarmingly precarious. When his heroic fury is aroused he suffers what Thomas Kinsella has called his "warp-spasm." This condition, which earns him the sobriquet "The Distorted One" first occurs in "The Boyhood Deeds," and is described at length in a later passage which begins:

> Then a great distortion came upon Cú Chulainn so that he became horrible, many-shaped, strange and unrecognizable. All the flesh of his body quivered like a tree in a current or like a bulrush in a stream, every limb and every joint, every end and every member of him from head to foot. He performed a wild feat of contortion with his body inside his skin [. . .]. (187; K 150)

Cú Chulainn is in many respects a man apart, but he is not altogether alone. For one thing, he has an important and multifaceted relationship with his charioteer, Lóeg, who saves his life on at least one occasion (179; K138). What I want to explore, however, is the significance of kinship in his performance of his heroic role, and it is time now to return to Medb's observation on kin-love that I quoted at the outset. This is made when she has contrived to persuade Fer Diad to take up arms against Cú Chulainn: she commends Fer Diad, saying "Every man has kindly feelings for his own people. So is it any more fitting for him to work for Ulster's weal since his mother was of Ulster, than for you to seek the good of Connacht, for you are the son of a Connacht king?" (197; K 170). In a way which is entirely characteristic of Medb, this is a rather perverse observation, since the preceding exchange between Fer Diad and Medb contains nothing to suggest that he is motivated by love for his people. Fer Diad seems rather to be solely concerned with his personal honor. It is out of fear of being satirized (and thus losing his honor) that Fer Diad responds to Medb's summons to him to go to the invaders' camp in the first place. He declines to go with the messengers she first sends to fetch him, and she then dispatches "poets and artists and satirists who might satirize him and disgrace him and put him to shame, so that he would find no resting place in the world until he should come to the tent of Medb and Ailill" (196; K 168). When he arrives at the camp, Medb's daughter Finnabair sets about seducing him and plying him with drink. Once he is suitably "sated and cheerful and merry" Medb asks him whether he knows why he has been summoned there. He effects not to know of any particular reason other than that it is perfectly appropriate for him to receive the hospitality that is being enjoyed by the other "nobles of the men of Ireland." She tells him that he has been summoned there so that she might bestow gifts upon him, gifts which she then lists, and which include great riches, enhanced status, Finnabair's hand in marriage, and Medb's sexual favours. Fer Diad, rendered sober perhaps by the seriousness of the situation in which he finds himself, divines Medb's true intentions (if indeed he was not already aware of them). He informs her that great as the gifts are he will not accept them from her as the price of fighting his foster-brother. In order to set him at odds with Cú Chulainn, she claims that he has boasted that he would defeat Fer Diad in combat. It is quite likely that Medb, who is no stranger to deceit, has made this up, but the alleged insult is enough to persuade Fer Diad that he must be the first to face Cú Chulainn in single combat on the following day.

Fer Diad's fierce concern for his honor is in keeping with the social code that informs the *Táin*. In the "Boyhood Deeds," Cú Chulainn goes so far as to say, "Provided I be famous, I am content to be only one day on earth" (143; K 85). But Fer Diad differs from Cú Chulainn in that his defense of his honor seems to be entirely self-centered, whereas Cú Chulainn's fame is acquired by dint of his defense of Ulster, and in particular of his own homeland, Mag Muirthemne. Moreover, Fer Diad's tragedy is that, having been told by Medb that his foster-brother has spoken ill of him, he feels obliged to redeem his honor in a way that, in the event, leads to his death. For Cú Chulainn, once he has heard that Fer Diad is to oppose him, does indeed make the kind of boast Medb has imputed to him: "I swear the oath of my people that his every joint and limb will bend beneath my sword-point as pliantly as a rush in mid-stream, if he once appears before me on the ford" (200; K 173). This, however, is not spoken as a challenge to Fer Diad. It is rather a response to Fer Diad's challenge to him, which arises only because Fer Diad has been foolish enough to take heed of Medb. Cú Chulainn makes good his boast and slays Fer Diad at the ford.

Following her observation on the universality of kin-love, Medb asks, "So is it any more fitting for him to work for Ulster's weal since his mother was of Ulster, than for you to seek the good of Connacht, for you are the son of a Connacht king?" This rhetorical question shows a form of litotes, so that it actually implies that it is more fitting for Fer Diad, who is the son of a Connacht king, to work for the good of Connacht, than it is for Cú Chulainn, who is related to the people of Ulster through his mother, to work for the good of Ulster. Just as Medb overstates Fer Diad's loyalty to his father's people, she gravely underestimates Cú Chulainn's devotion to his maternal kindred. When the future hero arrives in Emain Macha to join the boys, he announces to Conchobor that he is the son of Súaltaim and of Conchobor's sister Deichtine and indicates that he expects to be treated accordingly. He develops a close relationship with Conchobor, and the Ulstermen generally have a special affection for him because of his mother. Cú Chulainn, for his part, shows his loyalty to Conchobor in his deeds, but he also expresses it in his words. When an emissary comes to offers terms to Cú Chulainn, he identifies himself to the emissary only as someone who acknowledges Conchobor as lord; and when he hears the terms that would be offered he says that Cú Chulainn "will not exchange his mother's brother for another king" (160; K 116).

Yet, in her own way, Medb unerringly puts her finger on what ultimately determines the outcome of the struggle, when she says that "every man has kindly feelings for his own people." In the Irish text, this concept is conveyed by the adjective *condolb* which, according to the Royal Irish Academy's *Dictionary of the Irish Language* (DIL) means "mindful of kin, kindly" and which in essence has to do with love of one's kind (in its original sense). The same can of course be said of the abstract, *condalbae*, defined in DIL as "affection for kindred, love, sympathy, kindness," and which has also been variously translated "kin-love" and "feelings of patriotism." We shall see that the text is quite explicit in stating that *condalbae* underlies the response of the Ulstermen to the assault on their province.

The asymmetry in the contest between Ulster and Connacht is offset to a degree by the presence among the invaders of a group of Ulster exiles. A good half of the description of the muster of the invading army is devoted to the arrival at Rathcroghan of Conchobor's son Cormac Conn Loinges. His sobriquet Conn Loinges means "head of the exiled forces," but Fergus is much the most commanding figure among the Ulster exiles in the *Táin*. The reason for their departure from Ulster is explained in one of the 'prefatory tales,' which is entitled "The Exile of the Sons of Uisliu," but is often popularly referred to as "The Deirdre Story": it has to do with the violation by Conchobor of solemn guarantees of safe conduct given by Fergus and Cormac Conn Loinges. When Conchobor meets Fergus in the battle at the end of the *Táin*, he taunts him by identifying himself as "'One who drove you into exile to dwell with wolves and foxes, one who today will hold you at bay in the presence of the men of Ireland by dint of his own prowess'" (234; K 247). Fergus, for his part, claims responsibility for the raid in an address to Cú Chulainn: "'It was I who, in requital for the wrong done to me by the Ulstermen, collected and brought these forces to the east. With me the heroes and the warriors came from their own lands'" (200; K 174).

Fergus and his fellow-exiles are a constant presence in the invading army. When they have all set up camp at Cúil Silinne—the first stop on their eastward journey—the four men who share Ailill's tent are all exiled Ulstermen. We are soon reminded of their independent status when Fergus intervenes in a row that has developed between Ailill and Medb. Having conducted a survey of the army,

Medb tells Ailill and Fergus that one of the divisions, the Gailióin, has set up camp and conducted its business more efficiently than any of the others. She expresses the view that it would be pointless for the rest of them to proceed with the raid if the Gailióin were also to go, "for it is they who will take credit for the victory of the army" (129; K 66). Nor is she content that they should stay behind. She demands that they be killed. Ailill denounces this as "a woman's counsel," but Fergus responds more forcefully, saying, "It shall not happen unless we are all killed, for they are allies of us Ulstermen." Medb claims that she could do it in any case, since she has her own two divisions and the seven divisions of her sons, but once again Fergus is resolute in his response: "'That will not be,' said Fergus, 'There are here seven kings from Munster allies of us Ulstermen, and a division with each king. I shall give you battle in the middle of the encampment where we now are, supported by those seven divisions, by my own division and by the division of the Gailióin'" (130; K 66-67).

As it happens, no blood is shed over this matter: Fergus resolves it by proposing that the division of the Gailióin should be broken up and distributed among the other divisions, and Medb is content with that. Fergus has nevertheless made it clear that as an Ulsterman, he has a mind of his own, and the strength to back it up. We can now see that when Fergus said to Cú Chulainn that it was he who "collected and brought these forces to the east," it was not altogether an idle boast, especially if we interpret it in the light of his further observation that with him "the heroes and warriors came from their own lands." He is effectively the commander of that half of the army that is not from Connacht: the Ulster exiles, the Gailióin from Leinster, and the seven divisions of Munstermen. The significance of this is seen in the final battle: when Fergus and his division withdrew from the fray, "the men of Leinster and the men of Munster went away too, and nine divisions, those of Medb and of Ailill and of their seven sons, were left in the battle" (236; K 249).

Fergus is given the task of guiding the raiders to their destination. At first he leads them astray, and as we have seen, he sends a warning to the Ulstermen. In the first instance in the tale of a narratorial intrusion telling us what motivates one of the characters, we learn that Fergus sent the warning *ar chondalbi* "for the sake of kinship" (131; "old friendship" K 68). Another such intrusion quickly follows: "Then Fergus was given the task of leading the army along the path. He went far astray to the south to give the Ulstermen time to complete the mustering of their army. This he did out of affection for his own kin (*ar chondailbi*)" (131; "old friendship" K 69). Ailill and Medb notice that they are taking a strange route, and they begin to fear that Fergus will betray them. Medb tells him that he should no longer lead them if he feels the pull of kinship (*condailbi*), and he indignantly denies that there is any hint of treachery in what he is doing: the purpose of the detour is to avoid Cú Chulainn, "the great one who guards Mag Muirtemne."

The invaders cannot avoid Cú Chulainn for long. When they do meet, Fergus acts as intermediary between them, and we are in no doubt as to where Fergus's true sympathies lie. Let me give as an example Fergus's reaction to what happens when Cú Chulainn is fighting Lóch Mac Mo Femis. The Morrígan comes to Cú Chulainn in the form of an eel that twines itself round his feet so that he falls prostrate athwart the ford, allowing Lóch to inflict injuries upon him. Fergus is aghast at Cú Chulainn's performance, and he commands that one of his own men taunt Cú Chulainn "lest he fall in vain" (180; K 135). This is duly done, and Cú Chulainn is sufficiently re-energized to defeat Lóch.

The conduct of warfare in the *Táin* is governed by a set of conventions or code of conduct known collectively as *fír fer*, literally "the truth of men," but usually translated "fair play." This is frequently mentioned, but not always observed, in the *Táin*. On one occasion when the terms of fair play were broken against Cú Chulainn, Fergus, we are told, "demanded of his sureties that Cú Chulainn should get fair play" (182; K 139). This is evidently a demand, with the force of law, that in their conflict with Cú Chulainn, Fergus's Connacht allies act according to the conventions of *fír fer*, and for a time they actually do so—until Medb again loses patience and sends a hundred men to attack Cú Chulainn.

Of the many meetings between Cú Chulainn and Fergus in the *Táin*, the most significant is that which happens when Fergus has supposedly been persuaded to engage the younger man—here said to be his foster-son—in single combat. It is quite clear from their conversation on that occasion that neither one of them has the slightest intention of fighting the other. But a certain formality must be observed:

> "Retreat a step from me, Cú Chulainn."
> "You in turn will retreat before me," said Cú Chulainn.
> "Even so indeed," answered Fergus.
> Then Cú Chulainn retreated from Fergus as far as Grellach Dolluid so that on the day of the great battle Fergus might retreat before him. (194; K 165)

When Fergus confronts his old enemy, Conchobor, in the battle, he is understandably out for vengeance. The successive pleas of three of his fellow Ulstermen persuade him to stay his hand. His companion in exile, Conchobor's son, Cormac Conn Loinges, grasps his arm, as he is about to aim a vengeful blow at Conchobor. He begs Fergus to remember the honor of Ulster: "it will not be lost unless it be through your fault today" (235; K 248). Fergus turns aside, and Conchobor leaves the scene. Fergus nevertheless goes on to kill a hundred Ulstermen, and then he meets another of his fellow-exiles, Conall Cernach. Conall upbraids him for following a "wanton woman" and exerting force against his own "people and race." On Conall's advice he turns his sword on the hills, and with three blows shapes what are now "the flat-topped hills of Meath." These great blows alert Cú Chulainn and he approaches Fergus. He declares himself to be Cú Chulainn son of Súaltaim and son of Conchobor's sister, and he demands that Fergus hold back from him. Fergus agrees to do so, thus redeeming the promise he made when Cú Chulainn declined to encounter him in single combat (236; K 249).

Cú Chulainn owes much to Fergus and to others among the other Ulster exiles that are ostensibly his enemies. He is also assisted by the interventions of his human father, Súaltaim, and of his divine father, Lug. Both of them intervene sparingly, Súaltaim making two appearances, Lug only one; but each of them in his way profoundly affects the course of events.

Lug comes to Cú Chulainn from one of the habitations of the gods, which in Irish are called *síde* (singular *síd*), and which O'Rahilly here translates as "fairy mounds" (183; K 142). He brings him the balm of sleep, and he cures him of his wounds. He stiffens his son's resolve for battle by reciting an incantation beginning, "Arise, O son of mighty Ulster now that your wounds are healed."

While the hero sleeps, the youths of Ulster come south from Emain Macha to fight the invaders. They fight bravely and well, but in the end they are all slain. Cú Chulainn is dismayed when he hears about the death of the youths: "Alas that I was not in my full strength, for had I been, the youths would not have fallen as they did, nor would Fallamain have fallen." Lug consoles him as follows: "Fight on, little Cú, it is no reproach to your honour, no disgrace to your valour." But when Cú Chulainn invites him to stay, so that together they might avenge the boys:

> "Indeed I shall not stay," said the warrior, "for though a man do many valorous and heroic deeds in your company, the fame and glory of them will redound not on him, but on you. Therefore I shall not stay. But exert your valour, yourself alone, on the hosts, for not with them lies any power over your life at this time." (185; K 147)

Lug gives expression here to the heroic ideal, which is the exercise of valour in the pursuit of honor and fame and glory; in this he echoes Cú Chulainn's avowed commitment to the pursuit of fame. We might also find it unsettlingly reminiscent of Medb's reasoning with regard to the Gailióin: as we have seen, she demanded that they be put to death, for otherwise they would claim credit for the invading army's victory. Medb, however, was concerned with the collective conduct of a division in an army, whereas Lug and Cú Chulainn are focused on the single warrior. The distinctive attitudes of Lug and Cú Chulainn have to do with different loyalties. Lug has no interest in Ulster; his concern is for the welfare of his son. Cú Chulainn, on the other hand, is unswerving in his loyalty to his mother's brother and the province of which he is king.

Cú Chulainn's defense of Ulster is framed by two interventions on Súaltaim's part, both of which are described as warnings." The first occurs when Cú Chulainn and Súaltaim have received Fergus's message about the forthcoming invasion. Cú Chulainn asks his father to take a warning to the Ulstermen, while he himself sets about delaying the invaders. We hear nothing further of this first warning of Súaltaim's to the Ulstermen. We might well ask ourselves why Cú Chulainn should have dispatched him at all, given that Súaltaim and himself are the only two Ulstermen who are not stricken by the debility. There seems to be no point in delivering a warning to persons who are in no position to act upon it.

The answer I think lies in what we are told about Súaltaim's second appearance, which is recounted in the section entitled "The Repeated Warning of Súaltaim." This occurs as Cú Chulainn lies prostrate from his wounds which were such that "there was not on Cú Chulainn's body a spot which the tip of a rush could cover which was not pierced, and even his left hand which the shield protected bore fifty wounds" (217; K 218). Súaltaim has returned to his abode in Mag Muirthemne when he has intimations of an assault upon Cú Chulainn. He cries out: "Is it the sky that cracks, or the sea that overflows its boundaries, or the earth that splits, or is it the loud cry of my son fighting against odds?" He then goes to Cú Chulainn, who for all his wounds, is not pleased to see his father, for he knows that Súaltaim "would not be strong enough to avenge him." So he immediately sends his father off to Emain to deliver a message to the Ulstermen. We can assume that on the earlier occasion as well, Cú Chulainn sends his father away in the knowledge that he should not be expected to take a fighting role.

The charge given to Súaltaim on the second occasion is of the utmost seriousness: "'Go to the men of Ulster,' said Cú Chulainn, 'and let them give battle to the warriors at once. If they do not, vengeance will never be taken on them'" (217; K 218). Súaltaim goes to Emain and cries out: "Men are slain, women carried off, cattle driven away." In what is clearly a ritual, he shouts out this warning in three different parts of the court. A druid asks, "Who carries them off? Who drives them? Who slays them?" Súaltaim's answer to these questions is a succinct, if chilling, summary of what has happened so far in the *Táin*:

> "Ailill mac Máta slays them, carries them off, drives them away, with the guidance of Fergus mac Róig," said Súaltaim. "Your people have been harassed as far as Dún Sobairche. Their cows, their women-folk, and their cattle have been carried off. Cú Chulainn has not let them come into Mag Muirthemne and Crích Rois during the three months of winter. Bent hoops (of wood) hold his mantle (from touching him). Dry wisps plug his wounds. He has been wounded and bled profusely." (217; K 219)

The druid accuses him of inciting the king and says that he should die for it; the king concurs with the druid in this sentence, and the people concur with the king. With regard to the substance of Súaltaim's warning, however, the king adjudges him to have spoken the truth.

In view of the urgency of his mission, we might well expect Súaltaim to be appalled at the lugubrious pace of this quasi-juridical procedure. He is in any case dissatisfied with the answer he has got; he rushes forth, and falls on to his shield, the scalloped rim of which cuts off his head. He has apparently been attempting to flee Emain on horseback, for we are told that his horse brought the head back into Emain on the shield. In a final dramatic act, Súaltaim's severed head utters the same warning once more.

In Conchobor's response, Súaltaim is at once maligned and vindicated: "'Too loud was that shout indeed,' said Conchobor. '(I swear by) the sea before them, the sky above them, the earth beneath them that I shall restore every cow to its byre and every woman and boy to their homes after victory in battle'" (217; K 219). He is critical of Súaltaim's shout, but he unwittingly echoes Súaltaim's portentous words about the sky, the sea and the earth, and he vows to act. True to his word, he immediately sets about the muster of the men of Ulster. Súaltaim's warning has the desired effect, and the wrongs inflicted upon Ulster and upon its defender, Súaltaim's own son, will soon be avenged in battle.

Each of the characters in this epic subsists in a complex web of alliances and relationships, and this affects their actions at crucial times. The contest between Ulster and Connacht takes place within the framework of a code of conduct which, as I have said, is frequently mentioned, but often breached. Rules of engagement are agreed, and ad hoc arrangements of one kind and another are made from time to time. Medb and Ailill have gathered a mighty army, with allies from Ulster, Leinster and Munster, as well as their own province of Connacht. Cú Chulainn in his defense of Ulster shows all the virtues of the martial hero—courage, ingenuity, physical prowess—in abundance. When all is said and done, however, it is the power of kin-love among the Ulstermen that brings them victory in this epic.

In the translation of Medb's statement implying that it would be more fitting to work for the good of one's paternal rather than one's maternal kin, "more fitting" translates the comparative of *cóir*, a word which has a strong legal resonance. It is worth noting that, in law at least, the paternal kindred would generally command one's primary loyalty in early Ireland. What stands to Conchobor in the *Táin* is that he is supported by those who are related to him through their mothers as well as those who are Ulstermen in the male line, and I shall close with a quotation which gives expression to this point. In what is perhaps the most touching passage of all in the *Táin*. Fergus describes the arrival on the scene of the final battle of Erc, son of Cairbre Nia Fer and of Conchobor's daughter:

"Without asking permission of his father, that boy has come to the assistance of his grandfather. It is because of that lad that you will be defeated in battle. He will experience neither dread nor fear as he makes for you in the middle of your army. Bravely will the warriors of Ulster roar as they hew down the army before them, rushing to rescue their beloved lad. They will all feel the ties of kinship (*condolba*) when they see the boy in that great conflict. Like the baying of a bloodhound will be heard the sound of Conchobor's sword as he comes to the boy's rescue. Cú Chulainn will cast up three ramparts of (dead) men about the battle as he rushes towards the little lad. Mindful of their kinship with the boy (*condalb*), the warriors will attack the vast (enemy) host" (228; K 234-5).

Tomás Ó Cathasaigh
Harvard University

Note

1. All quotations are from Cecile O'Rahilly, *Táin Bó Cúailnge: Recension I* (Dublin: Dublin Institute for Advanced Studies, 1976); references in brackets are to the pages of her book, followed in each case by references to the corresponding page in Thomas Kinsella's translation of *The Táin* (Oxford: Oxford University Press, 1970).

Recent Translations of the Táin Bó Cúailnge

The *Táin* has come down to us in various forms in the manuscripts. The oldest extensive form of it that survives is known as the first recension. This was put together, probably in the eleventh century, from a number of different sources. It has been edited and translated by Cecile O'Rahilly, *Táin Bó Cúailnge: Recension I* (Dublin: Dublin Institute for Advanced Studies, 1976), and it forms the basis of Thomas Kinsella, *The Táin* (Oxford: Oxford University Press, 1970). Kinsella also translates some of the prefatory tales, and the opening section of the second recension. The full text of the latter will be found in Cecile O'Rahilly, *Táin Bó Cúalnge from the Book of Leinster* (Dublin: Dublin Institute for Advanced Studies, 1967).

Suggestions for Further Reading

Gantz, Jeffrey. *Early Irish Myths and Sagas*. Harmondsworth: Penguin, 1981.

Greene, David. "*Táin Bó Cuailnge*." In *Irish Sagas*, edited by Myles Dillon, pp. 94–106. Dublin: Stationary Office, 1959.

Hiltebeitel, Alf. "Brothers, Friends and Charioteers: Parallel Episodes in the Irish and Indian Epics." In *Homage to Georges Dumézil*, edited by Edgar Polomé. Washington, D.C.: Journal of Indo-European Studies, 1982, pp. 85–111.

Kelly, Patricia. "The Táin as Literature." In *Aspects of the Táin*, edited by J. P. Mallory, pp. 69-102. Belfast: December Publications, 1992.

Mallory, J. P. 'The World of Cú Chulainn: The Archaeology of Táin Bó Cúailnge." In *Aspects of the Táin*, edited by J. P. Mallory, pp. 103–59. Belfast: December Publications, 1992.

Mallory, J. P. and Stockman, G., eds. *Ulidia*. Belfast: December Publications, 1994.

Nagy, Joseph Falaky. "Daring Young Men in their Chariots." In *A Celtic Florilegium*, edited by Kathryn A. Klar, pp. 144–51. Lawrence, Massachusetts: Celtic Studies Publications, 1996.

Ó Cathasaigh, Tomás. "Mythology in Táin Bó Cúailnge." In *Studien zur Táin Bó Cúailnge*, edited by H. L. C. Tristram, pp. 114–32. Tübingen: G. Narr, 1993.

Ó hUiginn, Ruairí. 'The Background and Development of *Táin Bó Cúailnge*." In *Aspects of the Táin*, edited by J. P. Mallory, pp. 29–67. Belfast: December Publications, 1992.

O'Leary, Philip. 'Fír Fer: An Internalized Ethical Concept in Early Irish Literature?' *Éigse* 22 (1987): 1–14.

Sayers, William. "Contracting for Combat: Flyting and Fighting in *Táin Bó Cúailnge.*" *Emania* 16 (1997): 49–62.

Tristram, H. L. C., ed. *Studien zur Táin Bó Cúailnge* (Tübingen: G. Narr, 1993). Contains a valuable bibliography of the *Táin*, pp. 245–64.

Irish Pronunciation Guide

Many Irish words and names sound not at all the way they look. To complicate matters, Old Irish is likely to take a variety of forms in transliteration. Regardless, the following rules will prove helpful in pronouncing the names of characters and places in the Tain.

Consonants

Consonants in the initial position, i.e., at the beginning of words, are pronounced much as in English. Single consonants in the medial or final position, i.e., in the middle or at the end of words are pronounced as follows:

b = *v*at or sometimes *w*ed

c = be*g*

d = bo*th*er

g = ma*g*ic

m = *v*at or sometimes *w*ed

s (before a, o, or u, or, when final, after these vowels) = *s*un

s (before e or i, or, when final, after these vowels) = *sh*un

t = a*dd*

Double consonants and consonant clusters are usually pronounced as they would be in English, except for the following:

ch = Ba*ch*

ss = as s above

Vowels

a, ai = f*a*ther

á, ái = r*a*w

áe, ái = *ai*sle

e, ei, éo, éoi = g*e*t

i = h*i*t

í, íu, íui = *I*an

o, oi = h*o*t

ó, ói = b*oi*l

u, ui = c*u*t

ú, úi = s*oo*n

úa, úai = m*oo*r

Unstressed short vowels usually become softened to the sound of a in tun*a*.

Stress

Most simple words are accented on the first syllable.

Discussion Questions

What is the significance of this story's being set during Samain, the Irish New Year and the beginning of winter?

What is the nature of the gods or other-world beings in the *Táin* and in other early Irish literature?

What motivation is there for the cattle raid in the first or oldest recension of the *Táin*?

What are we to make of the character of Medb? Can we can catch glimpses of divinity in her?

What are we to make of Cú Chulainn's battle frenzy or warp spasm?

What does it mean for severed heads to be able to deliver messages and speeches?

It has been argued that the disaster presided over by Medb is presented as a misogynist commentary on the incapacity of women to lead men? Is there any evidence in the text to support this interpretation?

The *Táin* is likely to have been written down for the first time by monks. Have they left any discernible or surmiseable mark on the text?

Are Cú Chulainn's multiple physical deformities positive or negative, signs of favor or disfavor?

What role does kin love and kin loyalty play in the *Táin*?

It has been said that we as readers ought to take care to distinguish between what a story's narrator tells us and what a story's characters do. What are some of the rewards of such care for readers of the *Táin*?

Discussion Points

• The possibility that the Ulstermen's debility or torpor is at least in part a winter's sleep.

• The various reasons why warriors go into battle: fame, rage, honor, shame, bribery, fate, etc.

• The frequency with which warriors are plied with alcohol before combat.

• The roles played by women in the *Táin*.

- The enemy's head as fetish, perhaps reflected in the fact that nearly every mortal wound described in the text is delivered to the head.
- The half-divinity of Cú Chulainn, and the roles played by his two fathers, the one human and the other a god.
- The three functions displayed by Medb: sacrality, force, fertility.
- The character of Fergus and his original role as a god of virility.
- The pervasiveness of humor, often dark, in the *Táin*.
- The role played by seduction *in extremis*, i.e., as battle strategy, in the *Táin*.
- Possible classical and/or biblical influences on the *Táin*.

Points for Further Investigation

- Archaeological evidence supporting or challenging the picture of Iron Age Ireland presented in the *Táin*.
- The elusive and complex lineage of Cú Chulainn in early Irish literature, involving three different conceptions.
- The backdrop of myth, especially cosmogonic myth, in the *Táin*.
- The significance of certain numbers in the *Táin* and in Celtic tradition, e.g., the repetition of 3 x 50 for hosts of warriors or 3 for the number of pupils in the eyes of prophetesses.
- The place and role of women in ancient Ireland.
- The role of the bard and the chariot driver in Celtic culture, and parallels in other Indo-European cultures, including those of ancient Greece and India.

INDEX

A Concise Dictionary of Akkadian, 30
Abraham, 9
Absalom Absalom!, 67
Adhyatma-ramayana, 112
Alexander, 10
Alter, Robert, 2
Amar Chitra Katha, 105
And There Was Light, 80
Aristotle, 5
Ashoka, 10
Assurbanipal, 21, 36
Atrahasis, 26, 28
Auerbach, Eric, 57
Augustine of Hippo, 3

Bakhtin, Mikhail, 109
Balaramayana, 111
Benveniste, Emil, 10
Berlin, Adele, 42
Bible, King James Version, 61
"Bilgames and Huwawa," 32
"Bilgames and the Bull of Heaven," 27
"Bilgames and the Netherworld," 37
Blake, William, 5
Bowen, Elizabeth, 68
"Boyhood Deeds," 135–138
Burkert, Walter, 34

Carne-Ross, Donald, 79
Charter House of Palma, The, 58
Chicago Assyrian Dictionary, 30

Ciardi, John, 85
Commedia, 85

"Death of Bilgames, The," 32, 37
"Deirdre Story, The," 139
Dictionary of the Irish Language (DIL), 139
Dillon, Myles, 10
Doniger, Wendy, 10
Dostoyevsky, Fyodor Mikhailovich, 58
Duchesne-Guillemin, Marcelle, 37
Dumézil, Georges, 10

Egyptian Book of the Dead, 3
Enuma Elish, 38
Epic of Gilgamesh, The, 8
"Eulogy of Cú Chulainn, The," 135
"Exile of the Sons of Uisliu, The," 139

Faulkner, William, 67
Finkel, I. M., 35
Flaubert, 59
Frame, Douglas, 89
Freud, 110
Friar, Kimon, 87

Gardner, John, 20, 35, 41
George, Andrew, 24, 28, 30, 35, 37, 41–42
Goethe, 3
Gordon, Cyrus, 9

Hamilton, Leonidas
   Le Cenci, 19
Hamlet, 67, 113
Harris, Rivka, 27
Henshaw, Richard A., 31
Herodotus, 10
Hesiod, 9
Hill, W. D. P., 120
Hiltebeitel, Alf, 11
Hippocrates, 2
Homer, 4–5, 8–10, 80–81,
   83–85, 87, 89–90
"Hymn to Delian Apollo," 80

Iliad, 4–5, 7, 80–81,
   83, 85
Inferno, 85
Ishtar and Izdubar, the
   Epic of Babylon, 19

Jacob, 57
James, Henry, 59
Joseph, 57
Joyce, James, 59

Kamasutra, 107, 115
Kamban, 111
Kazantzakis, Nikos, 84,
   87, 89
King Lear, 69, 113
King Saul, 57
Kinsella, Thomas, 137

Lacan, Jacques, 31
Last Quest of Gilgamesh,
   The, 23
Lewis, C.S., 3
Longinus, 82
Lusseyran, Jacques, 80

Machiavelli, 59, 60
Mahabharata, The, 11
Marshall, Sir John, 8
Masoretic Text, The, 63
Milton, John, 5, 41
Mimesis, 58
Morson, Gary Saul, 109

Orlando Furioso, Jerusalem
   Delivered, 41

Parpola, Simo, 34
Pascoli, Giovanni, 87
Plato, 5, 10, 84
Poemi conviviali, 87
Pollock, Sheldon, 8
Possessed, The, 58
Powell, Marvin, 40
Pythagoras, 10

Ramacaritamanasa, 120
Rendsburg, Gary, 9
"Repeated Warning of
   Súaltaim," The, 143
Ross, Donald Carne, 79

Samuel, 2
Saul, 10, 58–62
Sîn-leqi-unninnī, 36
Smith, George, 19, 26
Solomon, 9
Spenser, Edmund, 41
Stendahl, 58

Tennyson, Alfred, 86
Terence, 4
Thompson, R. Campbell, 35
Tigay, Jeffrey, 42
Tolstoy, Leo, 59

Ultimo Viaggio, 87

Valmiki, 6, 105–107, 109,
    111–112, 119–120
Virgil, 5

War and Peace, 59
West, M.L., 9, 10
Woolf, Virginia, 59
Wu Men, 80

Xerxes, 10

Zeman, Ludmila, 23–24

ABOUT THE CONTRIBUTORS

Robert Alter is Class of 1937 Professor of Hebrew and Comparative Literature at the University of California at Berkeley, where he has taught since 1967. He is a member of the American Academy of Arts and Sciences and of the Council of Scholars of the Library of Congress, and is past president of the Association of Literary Scholars and Critics. He has twice been a Guggenheim Fellow, has been a Senior Fellow of the National Endowment for the Humanities, a fellow at the Institute for Advanced Studies in Jerusalem, and Old Dominion Fellow at Princeton University. He has written widely on the European novel from the eighteenth century to the present, on contemporary American fiction, and on modern Hebrew literature. He has also written extensively on literary aspects of the Bible. His eighteen published books include two prize-winning volumes on biblical narrative and poetry and an award-winning translation of Genesis. He has devoted book-length studies to Fielding, Stendahl, and the self-reflexive tradition in the novel. Among his publications over the past ten years are *The Pleasures of Reading in an Ideological Age* (1989), *Necessary Angels: Tradition and Modernity in Kafka, Benjamin, and Scholem* (1991), *Genesis: Translation and Commentary* (1996), and *The David Story: A Translation with Commentary of 1 and 2 Samuel* (1999).

Wendy Doniger is Mircea Eliade Distinguished Service Professor of the History of Religions in the Divinity School, the Department of South Asian Languages and Civilizations, the Committee on Social Thought, and the College of the University of Chicago. She holds the M.A. and Ph.D. from Harvard University and the D.Phil. from Oxford University. Doniger's research and teaching interests revolve around two basic areas, Hinduism and mythology. Her courses in mythology address mythological themes in cross-cultural expanses; her courses in Hinduism cover a broad spectrum that, in addition to mythology, considers law, ritual, art, and dance. Cross-cultural offerings have included courses focusing on death, dreams, women, evil, and horses. Among her many books published under the name of Wendy Doniger O'Flaherty are *Hindu Myths: A Sourcebook,* translated from the Sanskrit; *The Rig Veda: An Anthology, 108 Hymn,* translated from the Sanskrit; *The Laws of Manu,* with Brian K. Smith; *Women, Androgynes, and Other Mythical Beasts; Dreams, Illusions and Other Realities; Tales of Sex and Violence: Folklore, Sacrifice, and Danger in the Jaiminiya Brahmana;* and *Other Peoples' Myths: The Cave of Echoes.* Under the name of Wendy Doniger, she has edited *Mythologies*, an English-language edition of Yves Bonnefoy's 1,300-page *Dictionnaire des Mythologies*, and published *The Implied Spider: Politics and Theology in Myth; Splitting the Difference: Gender and Myth in Ancient Greece and India;* and *The Bedtrick: Tales of Sexual Masquerade*. In progress are a new translation (with Sudhir Kakar) of the *Kamasutra*, a translation of the final books of the *Mahabharata*, and a novel.

Alan D. Hodder is Professor of Comparative Religion and Dean of the School of Humanities, Arts, and Cultural Studies at Hampshire College. He holds the M.T.S. in the history of religion from Harvard Divinity School and the M.A. and Ph.D. in the study of religion from Harvard University, where he also served on the faculty before coming to Hampshire in 1994. His teaching interests include religion and literature in South Asia, American literary and religious history, myth and myth theory, and American Transcendentalism. He has written widely on such topics as Puritan pulpit rhetoric, Orientalism, American Romanticism, and the Bengal renaissance. He is the author of *Emerson's Rhetoric of Revelation* and, most recently, *Thoreau's Ecstatic Witness*.

Stanley Lombardo received his doctorate in classics from the University of Texas and has taught at the University of Kansas for two decades. His gripping and spirited translations of both the *Iliad* and *Odyssey* have sprung from the solo dramatic performances of Greek epic which he first gave in the early 80's. Eventually, these focused performance pieces led him to embrace and to recreate the entirety of Homer's great poems. Writing in the *New York Times*, Daniel Mendelsohn noted that "on nearly every page Lombardo provides some wonderful fresh refashioning of his (Homer's) Greek." Richard Martin of Princeton further remarked that "there are brilliant touches on every page.... Altogether this is as good as Homer gets in English." Lombardo's other translations include Hesiod's *Theogony* and *Works and Days*, the poems of Sappho, and, with Stephen Addiss, Lao-Tzu's *Tao Te Ching*.

John Maier is Distinguished Teaching Professor of English at the State University of New York at Brockport. After completing his graduate studies from the University of Pennsylvania and Duquesne University, Professor Maier pursued postdoctoral study in ancient Sumerian and Akkadian cuneiform and literature, as well as modern standard Arabic and Moroccan Arabic. In 1984, together with John Gardner, Professor Maier published a landmark translation of the Epic of Gilgamesh, which to a generation of scholars and students has provided illuminating access to one of the most stirring works of literature ever written. In addition to innumerable articles and papers, Professor Maier has published five books on the literature of the ancient Near East, as well as the modern Middle East and North Africa. These volumes include: *Myths of Enki, The Crafty God* (with Samuel Noah Kramer) and *Desert Songs: Western Images of Morocco and Moroccan Images of the West*. His rich and massive volume entitled *Gilgamesh: A Reader* is an invaluable companion to those who are tempted to turn the study of Gilgamesh from a diversion to a life work.

Robert E. Meagher is Professor of Humanities in the School of Humanities, Arts, and Cultural Studies at Hampshire College. With degrees from the University of Notre Dame and the University of Chicago, he held regular appointments at Indiana University, Bloomington and the University of Notre Dame before joining the Hampshire faculty in 1972. Across thirty-four years of teaching, he has held visiting chairs and professorships at numerous colleges and universities, including Trinity College, Dublin, Yale University, the University of Missouri, the University of Tennessee, and Willamette University. His publications include over a dozen books, as well as a handful of translations from ancient Greek (Aeschylus and Euripides) and several original plays. Alongside his scholarly work, Meagher has offered workshops on the translation and production of Greek drama for the contemporary stage at a number of colleges and universities, here and abroad, and has himself directed productions of Euripidean dramas at such venues as the Samuel Beckett Centre in Dublin and the Center for the Performing Arts in Kansas City, Missouri.

Tomás Ó Cathasaigh is the Henry L. Shattuck Professor of Irish Studies, and Director of Graduate Studies in Celtic Languages and Literatures at Harvard University. With degrees in English and in Early and Medieval Irish from the National University of Ireland, Professor Ó Cathasaigh was for many years Statutory Lecturer in Early and Medieval Irish at University College Dublin. He has written and lectured widely on early Irish myth and literature. His many publications include: *The Heroic Biography of Cormac mac Airt*, published by the Dublin Institute for Advanced Studies; "Between Man and God: the Hero of Irish Tradition"; "The Threefold Death in Early Irish Sources"; "*Cath Maige Tuired* as Exemplary Myth"; "The Sister's Son in Early Irish Literature"; and thirty-six entries in *The Oxford Companion to Irish Literature*.

www.ingramcontent.com/pod-product-compliance
Lightning Source LLC
Chambersburg PA
CBHW051102230426
43667CB00013B/2404